Biblical Foundations
Of
Psychology and Counseling

Christopher Cone, Th.D, Ph.D, Ph.D
Luther Ray Smith Jr., Psy.D

General Editors

Exegetica Publishing
2022

Contributors

Josiah Boyd, D.Min
Jeff Christianson, Ph.D
Christopher Cone, Th.D, Ph.D, Ph.D
Jeffrey Cox, D.Min
Allan Henderson, Ed.D
Luther Ray Smith Jr., Psy.D

Contents

1

Deconstructing Psychology

Christopher Cone, Th.D, Ph.D, Ph.D

THE MATTERS OF DEFINITION
AND ORDER OF INQUIRY

"Christians cannot trust psychology,"[1] says Ed Bulkley, but he doesn't leave it at that. Bulkley wisely clarifies that, "When speaking of psychology or psychiatry...I am referring to them in the counseling or therapeutic sense, which involves efforts to diagnose and change human behavior, thinking, attitudes, values, and beliefs through 'psychotherapies.'"[2] Bulkley further adds that he is not indicting "all forms of psychological research, such as those dealing with physical causes of psychopathologies, the physiological workings of the brain, or other non-value oriented studies."[3] A later reference is particularly helpful, as he narrows the scope of the problem from everything related to psychology to a particular kind of psychology, made evident in Bulkley's disagreement with the idea that "without the insights of secular psychology, pastors and churches are simply inadequate to deal with the deepest hurts of modern

---

[1] Ed Bulkley, *Why Christians Can't Trust Psychology* (Eugene, OR: Harvest House, 1993), 7.
[2] Ibid.
[3] Ibid., 7-8.

man."[4] While Bulkley at the first critiques psychology, as he writes it becomes evident that his contention is with *secular* psychology, not the discipline of psychology itself.

Greg Gifford illustrates the dichotomy in his article entitled, "Why biblical counseling and not psychology?" Gifford "affirms biblical counseling because we are committed to the Word of God as being authoritative Truth; because the only means of authentic change begins with faith in Jesus; and because the ultimate jurisdiction of counseling falls within the church. Our commitment to biblical counseling is an out-working of our commitment to these stated truths."[5] Early in Gifford's article, the problem is stated as psychology, but as he continues his explanation, it is clear that diagnosis is perhaps too general. Gifford adds, "biblical counseling is committed to the fact that in order to engage in psychology, one must be committed to the authority of God's Word to articulate the nature of the soul and human behavior! This is where the psychology of biblical counseling differs from secular psychology."[6] Importantly, Gifford recognizes that there is a psychology of biblical counseling.

John Street maintains the dichotomy as he laments, "The principles of psychology are presented as though they were on the same authoritative level as Scripture and compete for its jurisdiction as the sole authority in determining the well-being of the soul."[7] Note the dichotomy as being between the Bible and the principles of psychology. There is no third option in play here, in contrast to the conclusions evident with Bulkley and Gifford. Likewise, Jay Adams trenchantly asserts that the dichotomy is unbreachable, and that if the two options are brought

---

[4] Ibid., 24.
[5] Greg Gifford, "Why biblical counseling and not psychology?" February 27, 2018, viewed at https://www.masters.edu/news/biblical-counseling-v-pyschology.html.
[6] Ibid.
[7] John Street, "Why Biblical Counseling and Not Psychology?" in *Counseling: How to Counsel Biblically* (Nashville, TN: Thomas Nelson, 2005), 32.

together, the first option (psychology) is taken while the second (the sufficiency of Scripture) is discarded:

> Integrationist counseling seeks to combine the insights of psychology with those of the Bible…attempted integration of the Scriptures with worldly counseling beliefs, methods, and/or techniques inevitably means that in order to make them agree, the Scriptures are bent to fit the non-scriptural material that the counselor attempts to integrate with it. I believe the task is impossible without ending in a non-scriptural method.[8]

The first question that these observations elicit is simply *"What, in fact, is psychology?"* While Bulkley and Gifford at first condemn psychology in general, they later clarify that it is *secular or unbiblical psychology* that is actually the problem. Their clarifications illustrate that there may be a third option.

Psychology is from two Greek words *psuche* – soul, and sometimes mind, and *logos* – word or idea. Together the words communicate *the study of the soul and the mind.* As has been well communicated in other contexts, it is vital to recognize the difference between a discipline and a worldview. Psychology, for example, is a discipline – the study of the soul and mind. Any particular discipline is part of the pursuit of an accurate worldview. So, the outcome of psychological enquiry will contribute to one's worldview, just as what an interlocutor concludes about prerequisite worldview concepts will shape one's psychological enquiry.

To illustrate, in any worldview, one must first consider the questions of epistemology – how one might arrive at truth, how one might be confident of what is truth, and what basis of authority one can trust in order to ascertain truth. Then one must answer the key metaphysical

---

[8] Jay Adams "Competent to Counsel: An Interview with Jay Adams" from Tabletalk Magazine, February 1, 2014, viewed at
https://www.ligonier.org/learn/articles/competent-counsel-interview-jay-adams/.

questions – what actually exists, what is value and good, what is the purpose or design, and what is going to happen. In order to know that one has arrived at the right answers to the metaphysics questions, one must depend entirely on their epistemological conclusions. If one relies on their senses and experience as the answer to their epistemological questions, they will likely deny the existence of God and the soul, because their tools for measuring experience are limited to the physical realm. If on the other hand, one relies on human reason as the epistemological key, then they may or may not affirm the existence of God and the soul when the begin to address the metaphysical issues. This is the same in any discipline – one's metaphysic is undergirded by one's epistemology, and the ethics prescriptions arise directly from the metaphysics conclusions.

One of the mistakes often made in many disciplines is moving to prescription before an accurate description is understood. Consider, for example, the mechanic who upon hearing a slight rattle in the engine prescribes a likely expensive repair, when a closer examination might reveal that a screwdriver had been dropped into the engine area. Or consider the doctor who prescribes a medication because a particular malady is suspected, but not entirely verified. Often in such cases, the prescription either causes a negative reaction or possibly no reaction at all which might help correct the symptoms. Attending to the symptoms is important, but only with the proper understanding of causations or conditions.

In the same manner, there has been a great focus on the methods and tools of counseling, but perhaps not enough attention is being given in popular discussion to the *bases* of counseling that are rooted in the discipline of psychology – the study of the soul and mind. Consider that often we will hear the term "soul care." While we may greatly prefer it to the term "psychotherapy," lexically the terms are synonymous, and reference the treatment of the soul (and the mind). It is important to recognize that before we can engage in "care" or "therapy" *we must understand what a soul and a mind actually are.* While care and therapy are in the ethics aspect of worldview, having to do with prescriptions of how one should treat the soul and the mind, the actual definitions of the soul and the mind are necessarily within the scope of metaphysics enquiry. Before we can consider the prescriptions (ethics) we have to earn those prescriptions by addressing the descriptions (metaphysics), and before we can answer the metaphysical questions, we have to establish an epistemological basis for preferring one description over another. Hume says there is no soul. Nietzsche doesn't care if there is one, because we can't know for certain and we can't interact with it anyway. The Bible asserts that the reality of the soul is an undergirding principle of human life. Which is correct? What is our basis for preferring one description over the other?

CASE STUDY: DETERMINISM AND VOLUNTARISM

One particularly interesting and important metaphysical disagreement is between determinism and voluntarism. Determinism is the idea that people are not free to choose, but their choices are determined by (usually) external forces. Voluntarism is a competing idea that people are indeed free to choose, and that external forces are not definitive. In the deterministic system, humanity is governed by external forces – by environment and experiences, in the perspective of secularists, and by God or original sin, in the perspective of theists. On the other hand, in the voluntarist system, human free will rules the day for both the secularist and the theist. For the secularist, there is no God with which to be concerned, while the theist must restrict the activity of God to ensure that He never violates the laws of free will.

It is fascinating that the secularist and the theist can agree on so much once the false dichotomy between determinism and voluntarism is adopted. For the secularist, the devices of determinism are merely vehicles for independence from a Creator and the requisite human responsibility. The secular determinist considers that humanity is not accountable for one's actions, and the theistic response is not to counter the undergirding determinism, but rather to simply assert that it is God who does the determining. Likewise, the secular voluntarist argues that one is not accountable to a Creator, and has varying degrees of culpability for decisions, while the theistic response is not to challenge voluntarism, but rather the source of the free will, as if God has drawn a line in the sand He will not cross, so as to safeguard human free will.

In both cases, the foundational principle of determinism or voluntarism as the metaphysical undergirding is often not even considered. It is in this responsive dance (between secularist and theist), that secular theories of psychology assert human independence from God, while the theistic response is to refute the conclusion, but not the foundation itself.

Determinist	Secular – environment, experience Sacred – God, original sin
Voluntarist	Secular – free will, no God Sacred – free will, restricted God

Sigmund Freud[9] and B.F. Skinner, for example, were both overt in their determinism, though their responses to treatment in light of that deterministic foundation differed greatly. Skinner's determinism importantly serves as the very basis for the behavioral sciences. Skinner suggests that, "If we are to use the methods of science in the field of human affairs, we must assume that behavior is lawful and determined.

---

[9] E.g., Sigmund Freud, "The Psychopathology of Everyday Life," *The Standard Edition of the Complete Works of Sigmund Freud*, ed., James Strachey, et al, VI (London, 1953), 253-254.

We must expect to discover that what a man does is the result of specifiable conditions and that once these conditions have been discovered, we can anticipate and to some extent determine his actions."[10]

On the other hand, Thomas Szasz argues from the voluntarist perspective, acknowledging that, "My opposition to deterministic explanations of human behavior does not imply any wish to minimize the effects, which are indeed significant, of personal past experiences. I wish only to maximize the scope of voluntaristic explanations – in other words, to reintroduce freedom, choice, and responsibility, into the conceptual framework and vocabulary of psychiatry."[11] Jay Adams, the father of nouthetic counseling, appeals to Szasz repeatedly in *Competent to Counsel*, suggesting that based on Szasz' observations, "There seems to be little question, then, that much re-thinking is called for. And Christians ought to be foremost among those engaged in such re-thinking."[12]

While none should question the wisdom in Adams' challenge for Christians to rethink and to lead in that process, it is curious that he appeals to a secularist and a voluntarist to provide an impetus for progress in the discipline. It is also worth noting that as a Reformed thinker, longtime Presbyterian pastor, and full Calvinist, that Jay Adams would be most comfortable with the determinist versus voluntarist perspective, as the voluntarist approach would have been more compatible with an Arminian understanding of human volition and its relationship to God. The point here is that secular psychology is built on certain foundations, and only some of those foundations are being exposed by their theistic practitioners, while others are adopted without consideration. Ultimately, the issue is whether or not God has authority over His creation, and whether He has the authority to operate outside of the restrictions of

---

[10] B.F. Skinner, *Science and Human Behavior* (New York, MacMillan, 1953), 6.
[11] Thomas Szasz, *The Myth of Mental Illness* (New York: Harper, 1974), 6.
[12] Jay Adams, *Competent to Counsel* (Grand Rapids, MI: Zondervan, 1970), 4.

either determinism or voluntarism. But how would we answer this central metaphysical question?

DECONSTRUCTION:
PEELING BACK THE LAYERS OF PSYCHOLOGICAL INQUIRY

It is generally recognized that there are three divisions of history relative to scientific inquiry: premodern, modern, and postmodern. This threefold division considers the modern era, with Descartes' rationalism and Bacon's method, as its centerpiece. The premodern era was a time of superstition and unexamined beliefs, illustrated in the myths of the Greek pantheon. The postmodern era is a reaction to the failure of the modern era to deliver peace and prosperity through technology, as instead the modern era ended with the crash of world war and atomic destruction.

Roughly a millennium before the modern era began, Greek philosophers like Parmenides and Heraclitus began to lead Greek philosophy into naturalistic pursuit. The idea was that in order to find reliable answers, we must begin to examine the world around us and dispense with any ideas of the supernatural, instead preferring that which we can interact with – looking within the natural realm for our answers. The Greek naturalists were doing a form of science that was very limited, but their naturalistic presupposition would have great impact on forthcoming generations.

While these Greek naturalists were largely secular, later theists like Thomas Aquinas appealed to natural law as sufficient to offer us the metaphysical explanations we sought. Aquinas certainly recognized a Creator but modeled epistemological and theological methods that enabled one to look to the creation rather than to revelation for life's great answers. His *Summa Theologiae* showed how an entire theology could be developed absent a dependence on special revelation. The Protestant Reformation represented a return to the Text as the epistemological basis for answering the metaphysical questions, as Philip Melancthon in particular addressed issues of the soul and mind, and is credited as having a thoroughgoing psychology,[13] and perhaps even as originating the term, if Volkmann's assertion is correct.[14]

Descartes followed the Thomistic model rather than the Reformation example, with natural law rather than the Text providing the epistemological foundation for discovery, and with an acknowledgment of the Creator, yet with little dependence on His word, Descartes' rationalism and Bacon's scientific method won the day, and set the course of inquiry for the next four centuries. Now wisely, both men recognized the limitations of scientific inquiry and their rationalistic moorings, but the discarding of special revelation was comprehensive enough that as psychology developed, there was little call for considering Biblical foundations. As Galileo put it, "The intention of the Holy Ghost is to tell us how to get to heaven, not how heaven goes."[15] Galileo's comment illustrates the growing schism between science and the applicability of the Bible.

By the time Darwin arrived, there was an increasing number of people who viewed the Bible to be inaccurate pertaining to scientific matters, and Darwin's evolutionary suppositions continued to sway opinion particularly in the scientific community. For many, Darwin's theory provided the final naturalistic nail in the divine coffin. As Nietzsche would put it, "we have killed" God,[16] as this type of scientific

[13] Frank Hugh Foster, "Melancthon's Synergism: A Study in the History of Psychological Dogmatics" in *Papers of the American Society of Church History*, Volumes 1-2 (New York, Knickerbocker Press, 1889), 185-204.

[14] Francois LaPointe, "The Origin and Evolution of the Term "Psychology" in *Rivista Critica di Storia della Filosofia*, Vol. 28, No. 2 (APRILE-GIUGNO 1973), 138.

[15] Galileo Galilei, "Letter to the Grand Duchess Christina" (1615), translated and reprinted in Stillman Drake, *Discoveries and Opinions of Galileo* (New York: Doubleday, 1957), 186, reprinted in D. C. Goodman, ed., *Science and Religious Belief 1600-1900: A Selection of Primary Sources* (The United Kingdom: Open University Press, 1973), 34.

[16] Friedrich Nietzsche, *The Gay Science*, Walter Kaufmann ed. (New York: Vintage, 1974),181-82.

perspective made God unnecessary and irrelevant. As one clever soul put it, "The immaterial has become immaterial."[17]

It is from within this seedbed that modern psychology became prominent as a discipline. By that time Melancthon's and the other Reformers' influence had long been eclipsed by the naturalistic foundations of Darwin and Nietzsche. In the mid-nineteenth century, Wilhelm Wundt (1832-1920) worked to establish a physiological psychology that would be an interdisciplinary bridge between physiology and psychology, contributing to both. Wundt applied experimental and research methods used in physiology to the discipline of psychology, including inductive experimental science, and ultimately sought to develop a *scientific metaphysic* that would explain all aspects of spirit and mind as related to physical processes and stimuli.[18] In seeking metaphysical answers with empirical means, Wundt used necessarily limited methodology to search for answers that extend far beyond the capacity of naturalistic tools. Like the Greek naturalists long before him, Wundt was pioneering a discipline with a deliberately limited worldview without understanding what would be lost by shutting the door to the possibility of the extra-natural.

It is evident from Wundt's work that the problem is not in the discipline itself. Just as none would argue the importance of an empirical physiology, applying empirical methods to any inquiry has great value, as long as the subject can actually be observed. The problem arising from Wundt's program was the epistemological presuppositions that metaphysical truth can be arrived at through empirical means. That is not a problem with the discipline, it is deficiency in the worldview. Wundt, widely recognized as the father of psychology, brought a worldview to his

---

[17] Ted Elliot and Terry Russo, "Pirates of the Caribbean: At World's End" Gore Verbinski, Dir., Disney, 2007.

[18] See William Wundt, *Principles of Physiological Psychology*, Edward Titchener, trans., in Classics in the History of Psychology by Christopher Green (Ontario: York University), viewed at http://psychclassics.yorku.ca/Wundt/Physio/.

discipline, shaped his methods accordingly, and set the trajectory for all who would later engage the discipline. Wundt's presuppositions and worldview footsteps are shared by many later contributors to the discipline of psychology. Some later students of psychology would agree overtly with the worldview foundations of Wundt and would consequently not question the prescribed methodologies. Others might not recognize that Wundt and the empirical discipline he pioneered were directed by naturalistic presuppositions, and also would fail to question whether the assumptions and methods were too narrow.

Ivan Pavlov (1849-1936) observed what has been coined classical conditioning, providing empirical data to undergird behavioristic and deterministic ideas. Sigmund Freud (1856-1939) recognized that there were other major influencers like experience, culture, and environment that would shape the psyche. In studying those especially, he found the deterministic factors that he thought provided greater explanation. Jean Piaget (1896-1980) applied the same principles to developmental psychology, recognizing that the human psyche develops differently in early years. Carl Rogers (1902-1987) built on Nietzsche's self-focused existentialist ideas to encourage self-actualization and to minimize judgment. B.F Skinner's (1904-1990) behaviorism and operant conditioning were built on the same deterministic and materialistic premises as Wundt's ideas. Abraham Maslow (1908-1970) developed a human hierarchy of needs that attempted to account for the material and immaterial needs of humanity, but all within naturalistic limitations. Scores of other influential thinkers have pursued the discipline of psychology through the lens of the humanistic naturalistic worldview, and all arrive at similar results – not because they are engaging a wrongheaded discipline, but because they have engaged the discipline through the wrong lens.

The task for us is to acknowledge that the discipline can and must be engaged with a holistic perspective on metaphysics, recognizing that the *material* cannot provide comprehensive explanations if humanity is in fact also comprised of the *immaterial*. Further, if reality extends beyond the natural, then we must also be willing to engage the extra-natural, or the supernatural. If we are willing to recognize this foundational key, then we can and should certainly engage scientific pursuit, but should do so without discarding the Creator's voice. To be certain, the Creator's voice must be recognized as *the certain authoritative data on any subject*, if indeed He has created.

THREE OBSERVATIONS:
PREFACE TO FURTHER PSYCHOLOGICAL INQUIRY

When we deconstruct psychology, we observe three things. First, the discipline of psychology is, in itself, not at odds with the Bible, nor does the discipline necessarily disregard the authority of the Creator. Just as in any other discipline, the foundational premises will shape methodology, and methodology will shape one's understanding of reality. If one begins with the epistemological premise that God is the source of authority, and that His word is the authoritative communication of His truth, then, if one is being consistent, one will engage the discipline of psychology just like any other discipline – through the lens of the Scriptures, being totally subject to their authority. The discipline isn't the problem, incorrect premises and presuppositions are the problem. There is nothing inherently wrong with pursuing the knowledge of the soul and mind – in fact, such pursuit is necessitated in order to understand the work God does in sanctification and our connectedness to that work.[19]

Second, the discipline of psychology must first be descriptive, then prescriptive. The discipline attempts through various methodologies to observe influences and factors that shape the psyche. If one limits

---

[19] E.g., 2 Corinthians 12:15, 1 Thessalonians 5:32, Hebrews 4:12, 3 John 2.

methodology due to the wrong epistemological premises (as does the humanistic naturalist), then the descriptions will largely be wrong, even if there are many truths observed along the way. Further, it would be foolish to discard truths discovered in any discipline simply because their discoverers held to wrong presuppositions and employed limited methodologies. Truth is truth and discarding truth because of disdain for the one who discovered it or for the means by which it was discovered is akin to the logical fallacy of *ad hominem*. Gravity is gravity, whether Newton's beliefs align or do not align with ours. Newton didn't create the law of gravity; he simply discovered and considers the natural laws in place that affect gravity.

Still, the key limitation of (the science of) psychology is in its inability to offer prescriptions necessary to properly treat the psyche. Science can arrive at accurate descriptions (if the right assumptions and methodologies are applied), but prescription is another matter entirely. Just as science can teach us how to clone animals, for example, science cannot tell us whether or not we *should*. We must look beyond the scope of empirical science to help us with the ethical questions. A thoroughgoing psychology (a) must be built on proper epistemological foundations, (b) must accurately describe the reality of the human psyche and its relationship to the Creator, and (c) must arrive at proper prescriptions. Science, with its empirical limitations, *cannot* accomplish these three things. The discipline of psychology, by definition, then, must extend far beyond the empirical, or it will be insufficient at best, and totally misguided at worst. It cannot be *simply* scientific, but must include broader processes.

A third observation we must make in deconstructing psychology, is the absolute necessity of *reconstructing psychology properly*. We have observed throughout the history and development of psychology that many influential thinkers have worked from naturalistic premises. Consequently, the trajectory of the discipline has been largely limited to empirical observation and has been markedly anti-supernatural. Yet, if we have indeed been created, and if the Creator has communicated to us in the Scriptures, then we have been provided with the foundational principles, and the continually guiding truths upon which to properly ground the discipline of psychology.

In the case of our being the products of the Creator, we must look to our Creator to understand His perspective on who and what we are and how we are to care for Him, for others, and for ourselves. Soul care or psyche-therapy (or whatever else we may wish to call it) can only be rightly engaged when we get the descriptions and the prescriptions right. His word on the psyche, the soul, the mind, etc., is the first and the final word. "For the Lord gives wisdom; from His mouth come knowledge and understanding."[20] It is because of this universal truth that we are warned by the Apostle Paul to "see to it that no one takes you captive through philosophy and empty deception according to the tradition of men, according to the elementary principles of this world, rather than according to Christ."[21]

Philosophy according to the traditions of humanity – with limited humanistic perspective, and according to the basic (observable?) components of this world is simply empty deception. That philosophy keeps us in bondage. However, if on the other hand, our philosophy is *according to Christ*, that is no empty deception. *That* is not bound up in the basic principles of this world, limited by what we can observe in the various laws of nature. Instead, we discover there our freedom, because He is the way, the truth and the life, and no man comes to the Father but through Him.[22] He is the Creator who speaks to us with authority,[23] who

---

[20] Proverbs 2:6.
[21] Colossians 2:8.
[22] John 14:6.
[23] Matthew 7:29.

knows the design of humanity,[24] and is the ultimate standard of what we are intended to be like.[25]

If we fail to pursue that kind of philosophy, and the disciplines that stem from it, then we are relegated to be, as Joyce puts it, "the 'fallible man who attempts to speak authoritatively.' That man has always been with us, as both comforter and misleader, ever struggling to fit his rules around the oldest of mysteries—the one that Greeks called the psyche, cognitive scientists call the mind, and people of faith call the soul."[26]

---

[24] Psalm 139, Hebrews 4:12-13.
[25] Romans 8:28-29.
[26] Kathryn Joyce. "The Rise of Biblical Counseling" in The Pacific Standard, September 2, 2014, viewed at https://psmag.com/social-justice/evangelical-prayer-bible-religion-born-again-christianity-rise-biblical-counseling-89464.

2
Psychology: Discipline or Philosophy?
Luther Ray Smith Jr., Psy.D

Within fundamental Christianity there is a long enduring conflict concerning the issue of psychology and the place that it has within the church. Some believers are convinced the instructions and findings within psychology yields great benefits in resolving issues they believe the church can benefit. Others are persuaded psychology can be useful in specific situations (such as those who need objective medical care), but it produces nothing useful in terms of spiritual matters for the believer or humanity at large. It is also observed there are others who argue that psychology, and the teachings found in psychology, have no place in the body of Christ concerning human beings, the interactions among human beings, and that the Bible gives us all we need in addressing all the ailments of mankind.

These various positions that each group asserts depends on what each group believes what psychology is, and the purpose of psychology. The first group of believers who see psychology as beneficial may observe psychology as something to study and exploit the information it produces. The second group may observe psychology as something to be practiced in a specific context (e.g., the medical community), but in terms of spiritual truth one is instructed to be highly skeptical. The third group may see psychology as a set of teachings that are antithetical to the teachings that are found in Scripture and should be avoided. These various positions may cause one outside these groups to become ambivalent on what psychology is and its overall purpose. This inquiry will investigate a formal definition and explanation of psychology and philosophy, compare and contrast the implications of each explanation of psychology and philosophy. Then various Scriptures in light of the various explanations concerning the comparisons and contrast concerning psychology and philosophy will be observed. Lastly, a model of psychology, in light of the various Scriptures will be surveyed.

PSYCHOLOGY: A FORMAL DEFINITION

An etymological examination of the word *psychology* emphasizes the purpose behind this subject. The term psychology comes from the Latin word *psyche* (which derives from the Greek word psuche) meaning "breath, spirit, mind, or soul." The suffix of the word is *logia* is a word structuring component that is described as a study or a discourse of a particular subject. Concerning this particular word itself, psychology is the discourse or study of the mind or an individual. There are various explanations of this word that carry with it these specific ideas. Noah Webster gave his explanation on what psychology is when he commented that psychology is, "A discourse or treatise on the human soul; or the doctrine of the nature and properties of the soul."[1] Gregg Henriques gives a practical explanation of psychology when he expresses that psychology "is the science of mental behavior and the human mind, and the professional application of such knowledge toward the greater good."[2] Carole Wade and Carol Tavris offer a formal description of the word *psychology*, "as the discipline concerning with behavior, mental processes

[1] Noah Webster, *American Dictionary of The English Language*. Retrieved from https://www.webstersdictionary1828.com.

[2] Gregg Henriques. *Psychology Defined: What Exactly is Psychology?* Retrieved from https://www.psychologytoday.com.

and how they are affected by an organisms physical state, mental state, and external environment."[3]

Psychology, from the descriptions given underscores that it is a study and analysis of the human being, specifically the human mind and soul for the purpose of improving, or strengthening one's life behaviorally, personally and relationally. In addition, *psychology*, is also closely associated with the branch of *science*, which is described as, "the pursuit and application of knowledge and understanding of the natural and social world following a systematic methodology based on evidence."[4] According to the details of psychology observing the process of science is vital in understanding the patterns of human beings and human behavior. In short, psychology, concerning mankind and the aspects of mankind is "substance driven."

PHILOSOPHY: A FORMAL DEFINITION

The word *philosophy* derives from two Greek words: *philo*, meaning "love" and *sophia* meaning "wisdom." Philosophy, in short, means a "love of wisdom" and this love is driven by the quest for knowledge for the purpose of understanding existence. One institution highlights these points of philosophy in this manner,

> In a broad sense, philosophy is an activity people undertake when they seek to understand fundamental truths about themselves, the world in which they live, and their relationships to the world and to each other. As an academic discipline philosophy is much the same. Those who study philosophy are perpetually engaged in

---

[3] Cited by Bob Dushay, *Ask Dr. Bob*. Retrieved from
   https://www.people.morrisville.edu.
[4] The Science Council. *Our Definition of Science*. Retrieved from
   https://www.sciencecouncil.org.

asking, answering, and arguing for their answers to life's most basic questions.[5]

One such description not only attempts to describe what philosophy is, but the very purpose of philosophy when one writes the following:

> Philosophy is a way of thinking about certain subjects such as ethics, thought, existence, time, meaning and value. That 'way of thinking' involves 4 Rs: responsiveness, reflection, reason and re-evaluation. The aim is to deepen understanding. The hope is that by doing philosophy we learn to think better, to act more wisely, and thereby help to improve the quality of all our lives.[6]

Colin Brown gives his concise definition of philosophy when he writes that, "Philosophy is an intellectual discipline which is concerned with the nature of reality and the investigation of the general principles of knowledge and existence."[7] The qualities of philosophy, from the descriptions mentioned, is the pursuit of knowing truth (i.e., reality). Such questions that philosophy seeks to address are the following: What is knowledge? What is reality? Is there a God? What is good and evil? Why are we here? Why do we think? Etc. These questions, and many others philosophy observes, are not answered by merely gazing at the natural world but are resolved by affirming claims about mankind and the connection between mankind and reality logically and reasonably. To sum up, philosophy is concerned about the examination of life itself. Philosophy is "ideologically driven."

---

[5] Florida State University. What is Philosophy? Retrieved from https://www.philosophy.fsu.edu.

[6] The Philosophy Foundation. *What is Philosophy?* retrieved from https://www.philosophy-foundation.org.

[7] Colin Brown. *Philosophy & The Christian Faith*. (Intervarsity Press, 1968), 8.

PSYCHOLOGY AND PHILOSOPHY:
WHAT IS THE DIFFERENCE?

It would appear, at an initial glance, that psychology and philosophy are synonyms. However according to their definitions there are three ways that psychology and philosophy are distinct from one another. These differences are as follows:

1. Psychology, unlike philosophy, does not make presuppositional claims about mankind and the nature of existence. Psychology as a discipline is interested in observing the physical properties of mankind, the behaviors of mankind, and how those behaviors influence others. Philosophy, however, does make claims about reality and truth as it seeks to pursue the answers to the fundamental questions of what makes up reality and existence.

2. Psychology views mankind and the behaviors of mankind plainly. For example, when a researcher examines the human brain and how the human brain works in relation to the body this is a natural observation. The researcher may make a hypothesis about its workings, but the researcher does so by exploring the natural phenomena. Philosophy, on the other hand does not make observations from observable data, but rather *informs* the observer on how one is to examine reality and the world around them. For instance, if a researcher who is observing the human brain and its connection with the body, has concluded that over millions or billions of years the process of evolution has fine-tuned the brain/body connection, then this researcher's position on reality (i.e., philosophy) has informed him on *how* to look at the brain in relation to the body.

3. A discipline and philosophy can be recognized by its word forming ending that is associated with the overall word itself. For example, a word that ends with *ology* underscores a discipline (e.g., sociology, psychology, biology).[8] A philosophy can be recognized by the case ending *ism*, which highlights a particular set of beliefs and truth claims within a particular area (e.g., humanism, feminism, stoicism).

Psychology is a field of study and with it attempts to make sense of the inner workings of mankind and the interactions found within mankind. Philosophy does not observe humanity from a material aspect but does seek to understand knowledge, reality, and the nature of man's existence. Even though philosophy is not equivalent to psychology, one's philosophical position influences when one observes the findings in psychology (or any other field of study).

BIBLICAL PHILOSOPHY OBSERVED IN SCRIPTURE

One's philosophical positions are important in how one views and observes a particular discipline, which is seen in several examples of Scripture. One such example is King David, who in Psalm 19:1 wrote "The heavens are telling of the glory of God; And their expanse is declaring the work of His hands." King David was informed of this by his proper instruction of the Torah. Paul, spoke of David before he ascended to the kingship in the nation of Israel that God had said that David was a man after God's own heart.[9] This highlighted that David's philosophy was centered on the revelation of God in that it should govern

---

[8] Although this word ending *ology* is common among words in the English language this is not a strict rule. There are other words in that also describe areas of common study that do not have the ending *ology* (e.g., economy, astronomy, physics, etc.).

[9] Acts 13:22.

how he should observe the natural world around him. A similar observation of is made of King David concerning his own conception in the womb, which is described as follows, "For You formed my inward parts; You wove me in my mother's womb. I will give thanks to You, for I am fearfully and wonderfully made; Wonderful are Your works, and my soul knows it very well. My frame was not hidden from You, When I was made in secret, and skillfully wrought in the depths of the earth; Your eyes have seen my unformed substance."[10] David, observing some of the developmental characteristics of conception (i.e., inward parts, mother's womb, frame) to the personal handiwork of God Himself (i.e., "You formed," "You knit me," "wonderful are your works"). Once more King David's worldview was centered on the reality that God made the heavens and the earth, and this perspective was the lens by which he viewed human conception and growth.

This philosophical position can also be observed from King David's son, King Solomon, in the same attitude and character as his father,[11] and acknowledged the supremacy of God when Solomon asks for wisdom to guide the nation of Israel.[12] This wisdom is expressed in several books that Solomon penned in the Old Testament. In the Book of Ecclesiastes Solomon, in a "research study," observed some of the other philosophies under heaven by which one could believe and conduct themselves. He concluded, based upon these philosophies, and the wisdom they yielded that all of them he examined where vain and gave no satisfactory answers to life "under the sun." At the end of this book he concluded his research study with the following words, "The conclusion, when all has been heard, is fear God and keep His commandments, because this applies to every person."[13]

---

[10] Psalm 139:13-16a.
[11] 1 Kings 3:3.
[12] 1 Kings 3:6-15.
[13] Ecclesiastes 12:13.

This same viewpoint can also be observed in the Book of Proverbs where Solomon wrote the following statement, "The fear of the LORD is the beginning of wisdom, And the knowledge of the Holy One is understanding."[14] Within this book Solomon observed, and wrote the wisdom of how to make wise choices when living and conducting oneself in the world. The book of Proverbs addresses many subjects including proper marital relationships,[15] proper friendships,[16] proper attitude regarding labor,[17] how to be an effective leader,[18] how a child is to respond to their parents,[19] etc. All of these couplets of wisdom Solomon provided are governed over the philosophy of Special Revelation (i.e., "the fear of the Lord is the beginning of wisdom").[20]

This philosophy is also underscored in the New Testament. We see the Biblical philosophy highlighted when Paul lists his credentials as including his training in the Tanakh.[21] Writing to the saints in Rome, Paul observed that,

> the wrath of God is revealed from heaven against all ungodliness and unrighteousness of men who suppress the truth in unrighteousness, because that which is known about God is evident within them; for God made it evident to them. For since the creation of the world His invisible attributes, His eternal

---

[14] Proverbs 9:7.

[15] Proverbs 12:4, 19:13.

[16] Proverbs 17:17, 27:6, 27:9.

[17] Proverbs 13:11; 14:23.

[18] Proverbs 20:28; 29:4.

[19] Proverbs 20:20; 23:25; 28:24.

[20] It is interesting to note that "the fear of the Lord" that Solomon wrote that is the beginning of wisdom is directly connected to God's word. King David in Psalm 19:9 when describing the word of God mentions it as "the fear of the Lord." This is significant in that in order to observe creation, life, and have a proper conduct throughout life it is imperative to have a philosophy that is centered on "the fear of the Lord."

[21] Philippians 3:4-6.

power and divine nature, have been clearly seen, being understood through what has been made, so that they are without excuse.[22]

Paul wrote to the saints in Rome concerning the pagans that due to their not acknowledging God's attributes in creation they were suppressing the truth. Paul further explained that what is known about God is plain (or obvious) to them because God has created nature with the sole purpose of expressing His character and attributes, mainly His eternality, omnipotence, and transcendence. Paul further explained that when this is observed plainly, one can see that all that one sees before them further emphasized that all of nature has a Creator. When Paul wrote this argument, he wrote this in light of his Scriptural philosophy. Amazingly, in these very verses, Paul also made the case that those who reject a Biblical philosophy also actively deny what is plain to observe.

Paul continued to expand on this main point when he addressed the saints in Colossae. In his letter he penned the following words, "See to it that no one takes you captive through philosophy and empty deception, according to the tradition of men, according to the elementary principles of the world, rather than according to Christ."[23] Paul after making a case for the preeminence and supremacy of Christ then instructed the believers that in Christ (and the doctrines of Christ that are being taught during the apostles at this time), are all hidden all the treasures of wisdom and knowledge.[24] Paul further warned the believers not be taken captive through "the philosophy." Paul considered in detail what philosophy the saints in Colossae were to avoid: (1) the man-made rules that others make where they could evaluate their righteousness before God, and (2) the philosophical perspective that was promoted by

---

[22] Romans 1:18-19.
[23] Colossians 2:8.
[24] Colossians 2:3.

the Greek Stoics at this time.[25] All of these perspectives, Paul explained, were antithetical to the instructions of Christ. Paul in this text gave the saints of Colossae several warnings within this epistle: (1) That the philosophy that governed the age is counter to the teachings of Christ, (2) it is possible as a believer to be persuaded to exchange the instruction that Christ has given, (3) that one's philosophy is extremely important, as it is connected to what one believes and their conduct.

In addition, Paul – like David and Solomon – explained this information from the perspective of what God has revealed in His word, and it informed how Paul was to instruct the saints of Colossae. Paul also used his Scriptural perspective to critique and reject all of the other

---

[25] The Greek word Paul uses to describe the elementary principles is the word στοιχεῖον (pronounced *stoichion*) which describes the philosophical system that described to be infused into everyday life. One website described the belief as follows: "The Stoics believed that perception is the basis of true knowledge. In logic, their comprehensive presentation of the topic is derived from perception, yielding not only the judgment that knowledge is possible but also that certainty is possible, on the analogy of the incorrigibility of perceptual experience. To them, the world is composed of material things, with some few exceptions (e.g., meaning), and the irreducible element in all things is right reason, which pervades the world as divine fire. Things, such as material, or corporeal, bodies, are governed by this reason or fate, in which virtue is inherent. The world in its awesome entirety is so ruled as to exhibit a grandeur of orderly arrangement that can only serve as a standard for humankind in the regulation and ordering of life. Thus, the goal of humans is to live according to nature, in agreement with the world design." (Encyclopedia Britannica 2020). It is also recognized that Stoicism, as a philosophy was hostile to the teachings of Christ as an author stated when he wrote, "[Stoicism's] chief competitors in antiquity were: (1) Epicureanism, with its doctrine of a life of withdrawal in contemplation and escape from worldly affairs and its belief that pleasure, as the absence of pain, is the goal of humans; (2) Skepticism, which rejected certain knowledge in favor of local beliefs and customs, in the expectation that those guides would provide the quietude and serenity that the dogmatic philosopher (e.g., the Stoic) could not hope to achieve; and (3) Christianity, with its hope of personal salvation provided by an appeal to faith as an immanent aid to human understanding and by the beneficent intervention of a merciful God (Encyclopedia Britannica 2020).

philosophies which did not agree with God's word.[26] David, Solomon, and Paul are examples of those who observed creation, life, and purpose all from the lens of God's revealed word. Special revelation was the basis for their observations of the many topics they covered. They understood the things within the universe and on earth God has given mankind to observe and research. This also includes the human being and mankind's behavior. Humanity was created on day six when the Lord fashioned heaven and earth.[27] The act of God creating mankind included all of the physical, physiological, and cognitive qualities that are found in male and female. Just as the heavens and all of creation on earth speaks of God's handiwork, so does all the parts which humanity possesses. Additionally, the Scriptures speak of another aspect of humanity: the spiritual reality

HOW THE DOMINANT PHILOSOPHIES
WITHIN PSYCHOLOGY ARE NOT ENOUGH

There are two dominant philosophies that are found within modern psychology. One such philosophy is known as secular humanism. Secular humanism is defined as, "a nonreligious worldview rooted in science, philosophical naturalism, and humanist ethics. Instead of relying on faith, doctrine, or mysticism, secular humanists use compassion, critical thinking, and human experience to find solutions to human problems."[28] The philosophy of secular humanism seeks to understand the substance and purpose of mankind without supernatural explanation, and instead relies heavily on "science, philosophical naturalism, and humanist ethics." This explanation is associated with the second

---

[26] Acts 19:22-31.
[27] Genesis 1:27-28.
[28] Center of Inquiry. *What is Secular Humanism?* (2020). Retrieved from
   https://www.centerforinquiry.org.

philosophy that is found within psychology, and this is materialistic naturalism. Dallas Roark describes this philosophy in this manner:

> In an elementary way, naturalism may be defined as the philosophy that nature is the sum total of reality. There is nothing that is beyond nature with regard to a Supreme Being that is unseen. To adapt a phrase, what you see is what you get. But the definition above is too simple. Naturalism includes diverse modes of thought that range from materialism (the idea that matter only exists) to humanism (the view that man is the model of explaining reality).[29]

The main theorists within the discipline of psychology have work from a philosophical position that "God is not," and as a result they have made some inaccurate observations in regard to the human being. One such psychologist is Abraham Maslow, who is known as the "Father of Humanistic Psychology" and developed what has become known as the "Hierarchy of Needs." His core worldview rejected the reality that a God exists and instead considered Christianity (and other religions) to be nothing more as part of the temporal human experience when he said that,

> Religious quests, the religious yearnings, the religious needs themselves - are perfectly respectable scientifically . . . they are rooted deep in human nature . . . they can be studied, described, examined in a scientific way . . . the churches were trying to answer

---

[29] Dallas Roark. *Introduction to Philosophy*. (1982). Retrieved from https://www.qcc.cuny.edu.

perfectly sound human questions. . . The questions themselves were and are perfectly acceptable, and perfectly legitimate. . .[30]

Consequently, because he had a philosophy that rejected the reality of God, he observed mankind as just a temporal creature and that one's enjoyment and purpose in life comes from one acquiring knowledge:

> All the goals of objectivity, repeatability, and preplanned experimentation are things we have to move toward. The more reliable you make knowledge, the better it is. If the salvation of man comes out of the advancement of knowledge--taken in the best sense--then these goals are part of the strategy of knowledge.[31]

Furthermore, because of his work the origin of the evil of mankind as something that comes from ignorance of knowledge as he noted,

> Most people are nice people. Evil is caused by ignorance, thoughtlessness, fear, or even the desire for popularity with one's gang. We can cure many such causes of evil. Science is progressing, and I feel hope that psychology can solve many of these problems. I think that a good part of evil behavior bears on the behavior of the normal.

Abraham's Maslow's "God is not" philosophy influenced his theoretical orientation within the discipline of psychology. Abraham Maslow, in his most famous theory titled *the Hierarchy of Needs* attempted to detail what

---

[30] Kinnes Tormond. *Abraham Maslow on Religion, Values, Self-Actualizers and Peak Experiences.* (2019). Retrieved from http://oaks.nvg.org.

[31] Hoffman. *Abraham Maslow Overcoming Evil: An interview with Abraham Maslow, founder of humanistic psychology.* (1992). Retrieved from https://www.psychologytoday.com.

motivated mankind to conduct themselves in certain ways. These needs of mankind he outlined in sequential fashion: Physiological, safety, love and belonging, esteem, and self-actualization. Abraham Maslow was convinced that if a person was unsatisfied in his basic lower needs, he would not be able to address the higher needs as he described when he wrote the following, "At once other (and "higher") needs emerge and these, rather than physiological hunger, dominate the organism. And when these, in turn, are satisfied, again new (and still "higher") needs emerge and so on. This is what we mean by saying that the basic human needs are organized into a hierarchy of relative prepotency."[32]

Due to his plain observation of human behavior Abraham Maslow understood that mankind does have certain physical, physiological, and cognitive needs. However due to his worldview the solution for Abraham Maslow concerning the perils and purpose of man was found in fulfilling these physical needs. When one fulfills each of these physical needs eventually, according to Maslow, they will come to see themselves as significant and purposeful in the world. [33] Abraham

---

[32] Hoffman. *Abraham Maslow Overcoming Evil: An interview with Abraham Maslow, founder of humanistic psychology.* (1992). Retrieved from https://www.psychologytoday.com.

[33] There are two critiques that place the Abraham Maslow's theory *Hierarchy of Needs* more in the philosophical category rather than the psychological category: 1) According to researchers who observed the theory they stated there is no empirical support for this theory when they wrote " Maslow's Hierarchy of Needs theory is frequently uncritically cited in texts, even though most evidence has failed to support its validity. Science requires that theory be supported by empirical facts. Maslow's theory is briefly summarized, along with a review of the related literature. Reasons are given and empirically supported for the continued popularity of Maslow's theory in marketing despite lack of scientific support." (Barlow Soper, Gary Milford, & Gary Rosenthal. *Belief When Evidence Does Not Support Theory.* (Psychology & Marketing, 1995). Retrieved from https://doi.org/10.1002/mar.4220120505). 2) The one research study that was conducted concerning this theory was correct in terms of is observations concerning the objective needs of mankind. However, the researchers also concluded that "[the] happiest people were those who reported feeling fulfilled in most of those areas. But, contrary to Maslow, the sequence in which their "higher" and "lower" needs were met did not influence their sense of satisfaction or joy...[and that] a person can report having good social relationships and self-actualization even

Maslow observed the objective physical needs and interactions of people and used his "God is not" philosophy to inform him on what mankind is, and mankind's overall purpose.

However, the Biblical perspective revealed a holistic answer to who and what mankind is. The biblical philosophy acknowledged some of the natural observations of Maslow concerning mankind. For instance, when it comes to examining male and female and how they relate to one another these interactions highlight the invisible attributes of God.[34] When it comes to physiological and biological needs God provided for humanity's sustenance.[35] God provided the wisdom of how one should view themselves in light of creation.[36] God informed the individual of overall purpose in life.[37] Furthermore, God, through His word, underscored not just the material aspect of mankind, but also the spiritual quality of humanity,[38] a quality of that Abraham Maslow denies even exists because of his worldview commitment. God, in His Scripture also informed humanity of the origin of evil and the effect evil has had on the world,[39] and how evil has corrupted the essence and faculties of humanity and their experiences.[40] The word of God observed mankind as not only a temporal being but exists beyond the physical body.[41] Thus, it is the Biblical worldview that not only gives a comprehensive outlook for handling observable data of the natural world, but it also gives the

---

if their basic needs and safety needs are not completely fulfilled."(Good Therapy. *New Research Explores Accuracy of Maslow's Hierarchy of Needs*. (Good Therapy, 2011). Retrieved from https://www.goodtherapy.org). This once more observes that Abraham Maslow was asserting a truth claim about man's purpose and existence in the world from his physical observations.

[34] Romans 1:17-18.
[35] Genesis 1:29, 9:3, etc.
[36] Genesis 1:26-28, 9:7.
[37] 1 Corinthians 10:31.
[38] Genesis 2:7, John 3:1-7.
[39] Genesis 3:17-18.
[40] Romans 3:9-18; Ephesians 2:1-2.
[41] Luke 16:19-31; 2 Corinthians 5:6-7.

philosophy for understanding in the whole the substance of humanity and our purpose and destiny. Furthermore, the Scriptures informs the individual not just the physical properties of humanity, but reveals that humanity is at the core a spiritual being. In short, if psychology properly defined is "the study, discourse, or treatise of the human soul," then the Biblical worldview *is* the true psychology.

The Biblical worldview contrasts the anti-theistic philosophy found in many theorists and researchers within the discipline of psychology. The current mainline philosophy found in the discipline of psychology is centered on the idea that "God is not." Because of this perspective the observations that Abraham Maslow, and others who share this specific philosophy, may have insightful observations concerning some of the *physical* interactions of mankind and their ills. However due to the fact they lack the Biblical worldview (i.e., "God is") they often arrive at insufficient conclusions about the origin and substance of human beings, the ultimate purpose of relationships, the origin of malevolent activity, motivation for conduct, perspective about identity, and the overall destiny of mankind. Thus, if psychology is understood as observing the human soul and all of human attributes, then the mainline philosophy found within psychology (and by extension the practice of counseling) is incomplete and often woefully inaccurate.

CONCLUSION

Psychology is a discipline and not a philosophy or worldview. A discipline is a field of study (such as biology, sociology, geology, etc.) that observes phenomena in a natural state, using the scientific method to make and test plain observations about the natural world. A philosophy, or worldview, is a system of comprehensive ideas that inform us about reality. Philosophy is not a synonym for the discipline of psychology, but philosophy presides over psychology in determining how to view the natural observations found within the disciple. In addition, psychologists and researchers employing a "God is not" philosophy draw insufficient conclusions because the assumptions are wrong. Psychologists and researchers may make perceptive observations of human behavior and conduct, however, they may arrive at wrong conclusions about the purpose of humanity and the nature of humanity's existence because of philosophical precommitments, and not because of the discipline of study in which they are engaging.

The Biblical worldview expresses a true psychology, as it is the only perspective that observes both the natural and the spiritual properties of humanity – a duality that the "God is not" worldview rejects. In light of these details, the discipline of psychology (and by extension, counseling) is a subject that those espousing a Biblical worldview should not avoid. It is a discipline that belongs to God and should be studied by the people of God, for the glory of God.

Soli Deo Gloria!

3
Where Can Wisdom Be Found?

Jeff Cox, D.Min

Where can wisdom be found? Job poses this question in Job 28:12. The context of the question is a debate concerning his sufferings as recorded in what some scholars contend to be the first written book of Scripture.[1] The literary genre of the book of Job is a masterful poem, using the structure of Hebrew chiasm, where Job 28:1-28 forms the focal point of the parallelism.[2] While the theme of theodicy is a major emphasis of the book, the use of a chiastic structure argues that the author's intended purpose is an emphasis on wisdom.[3] Job argues in the immediate context of Job 28 that wisdom is elusive, hidden, not found in the land of the living with mortal humanity, and cannot be purchased. Instead, God alone knows the way to wisdom and where it dwells.

What is interesting is that in this great diatribe on wisdom, Job is arguing against the counsel of his companions. Much of the book is a counseling session. It can be argued that it is actually a demonstration on how *not* to counsel, for Job concludes that his companions are most

---

[1] David J.A. Clines, *Job 1-20: Word Biblical Commentary Volume 17* (Thomas Nelson Inc., 1989), 23-26.

[2] Tremper Longman III, *Job: Baker Commentary of the Old Testament* (Baker Academic, 2012), 127-28.

[3] Eliphaz the Temanite (Job 4:1) is considered by many scholars to be the author of the book.

miserable comforters.[4] God goes even further stating that Job's companions have not spoken truth concerning Job.[5] Nevertheless, the author's emphasis on wisdom contains a lengthy counseling session, arguing for a strong correlation between wisdom and counsel.

What is *counseling?* It would be impossible to come up with a definition that is all-inclusive, encapsulates every nuance of correct theology, and cannot be improved upon. However, if one begins with a construct that flows from the idea that there is a correlation between counseling and wisdom, one can arrive at some very helpful concise definitions.

The beginning chapters of the book of Proverbs contain counsel from a father to a son.[6] The initial goal set forth by the father is to know wisdom.[7] Later in the poetic narrative, the father summarizes and emphasizes to his son the purpose of his counsel: *get wisdom.* [8] The immediate context of the imperative argues for the preeminence of wisdom, the importance of wisdom, the attainability of wisdom, the rewards of wisdom, etc. The purpose of the father's counsel is summed up in the imperative: *get wisdom.*

The correlation between *counsel* and *wisdom* is readily apparent with even a cursory reading of Proverbs. The correlation strengthens to causation within the book of Proverbs as counselors are stated to provide wisdom.[9] This correlation/causation is consistent throughout Scripture. In the book of Ecclesiastes, Qoheleth[10] is sharing his counsel with the

---

[4] Job 16:2.
[5] Job 42:7.
[6] Proverbs 1:8.
[7] Proverbs 1:5.
[8] Proverbs 4:5.
[9] Proverbs 11:14, 19:20, 24:6.
[10] Meaning *preacher*, a self-given title for Solomon as he introduces the Book of Ecclesiastes.

understanding that wisdom will be realized and wisdom will be of value in one's life.[11] The purpose of counsel is to get wisdom.[12]

There are basic understandings found within Scripture that give a sense of the meaning of wisdom. The Hebrew idea of wisdom is more of a skill that produces value than merely a cognitive exercise.[13] Wisdom means generally, *masterful understanding, skill, expertise*.[14] This is not to imply that wisdom is void of any cognitive exercises, but the cognitive exercise is accompanied by actions, choices, discernment, value, etc. Wisdom can be learned, practiced, performed, and improved upon. It is a learned ability that results in the capacity to make right choices. Wise people choose to fear the Lord,[15] live in healthy community,[16] be teachable,[17] shut their lips, [18] and many other choices outlined in the book of Proverbs alone. Furthermore, wisdom produces value. Qoheleth argues that wisdom produces profit to those who see the sun, that is to those who

---

[11] Ecclesiastes 7:11-22.

[12] This is not meant to imply that wisdom, stated specifically, is the only goal of counseling to the exclusion of other benefits, i.e., the glory of God, conformity to the image of Christ, the will of God, etc. Too often false dichotomies are introduced into the discussion of counseling that pit ideas that are better understood as congruent rather than mutually exclusive or combative.

[13] The Hebrew word for wisdom, Chokmâh (לְחָכְמָה), carries the connotation of skill; in matters of war (Isaiah 10:13), administration (Deuteronomy 34:9, 1 Kings 3:28), and work (Exodus 28:3). It applies to both God's wisdom and the wisdom of man. The concept of volition and judgment is also associated with a Hebrew understanding of wisdom. The association of Chokmâh with ethics and morality imply that it is a moral skill that results in value. The idea of value is a concept developed by Qoheleth in Ecclesiastes. A pithy summary could define Chokmâh as skill in living with the purpose of producing value.

[14] Bruce K. Waltke, *The Book of Proverbs Chapters 1-15: New International Commentary Series* (William B. Eerdmans Publishing Company, 2004), 76.

[15] Proverbs 1:7.

[16] Proverbs 18:1.

[17] Proverbs 1:5.

[18] Proverbs 17:28.

are among the living.[19] Vanhoozer correctly observes the ultimate goal of Christian wisdom is to teach the individual to live well with others in the sight of God.[20]

If the goal of the father's counseling is intended for the son to *get wisdom,* then the goal of counseling is to *make one wise.* Summarizing the goal of counseling in this pithy statement does not mean that other goals and summary statements found within Scripture are incorrect or incomplete. To argue that the goal of counseling is to *make one wise* does not diminish the importance of other Scriptural goals, however, the direct correlation/causation between counsel and wisdom found in Scripture argues that *making one wise* is a straightforward stated purpose of counseling.

So what is counseling? Working from the purpose to *make one wise,* one can define counseling as *the process by which the counselor guides the counselee to become wise.* This definition is general and nuanced enough to not suggest specific approaches and preferences. One cannot inject one's own theological system, personal beliefs, and opinions into the definition. The definition is precise and concise enough to do justice to a straightforward reading of Scripture.

It should be noted that this definition does use the word *guide.* One could easily choose words such as *help, advise, direct,* etc. to define the technique of the counseling process. Help is an all-encompassing word that seems to share the spirit of counseling from Scripture.[21] It is a broad enough word to capture many different approaches. Words such as *advise* and *direct* seem to suggest a more commanding approach. This does not mean that imperatives are not consistently used in Scripture. However,

---

[19] Ecclesiastes 7:12; The author's use of the word וְיֹתֵר (profit) in Ecclesiastes comes from a root meaning "to remain over." While in the context of Ecclesiastes, this concept of profit is limited to scope under the sun, it does argue for value in this life.

[20] Kevin J. Vanhoozer, *The Drama of Doctrine, a Canonical Linguistic Approach to Christian Theology* (Westminster John Knox Press, 2005), 332.

[21] John 14:16.

the use of storytelling, asking questions, and teaching through the use of questions, hyperbole, poetry, parallelism, contrast and comparison, used throughout Scripture, seems to argue for a word that is more encompassing than different synonyms for an imperative. The word *guide* is a big enough word to encompass many facets of the counseling process.

So, if wisdom is skill in living, and the goal of counseling is to make one wise, and counseling is the process by which the counselor guides the counselee to become wise, another logical question follows: *Where can wisdom be found?*

This is a big question. Finding wisdom is a big endeavor. However, since the context of this narrative is counseling from a Biblical worldview, it would be remiss not to discuss some of the real and perceived differences within the Christian tradition of faith concerning counseling, specifically differences that exist within evangelical churches and evangelical learning institutions regarding counseling. By working through a definition of counseling that flows from an understanding of wisdom and the discovery of wisdom, it is hoped that many false caricatures, misrepresentations, and false dichotomies can be avoided.

Why the controversy? It is to be expected that there will always be a healthy debate when discussing what constitutes best practices in regard to helping people. How much more so when dealing with people in regard to the health of their mind, soul, and strength. When one seeks to provide guidance in these areas from a Biblical worldview construct, another factor is also injected into the conversation, which is the discernment to determine *godly* wisdom. James states that one should ask God for wisdom.[22] The Scripture also speaks of a contrast between the wisdom of God with the wisdom of this world. Paul attests to this reality in his correspondence with the Corinthians.[23] There is a wisdom that is not from God. These passages have a specific audience and context in regard to

---

[22] James 1:5.
[23] 1 Corinthians 1:19-31, 3:18-23.

wisdom and how it is acquired, but it cannot be denied that there will be a conflict regarding the *type* of wisdom one gets, ergo there will be a conflict with the issue of counseling. What is more difficult to determine is the actual conflict based on a proper understanding of Scripture and what might be contrived conflicts that do not find support in Scripture. Enter the counseling wars that have permeated traditions of faith for the past 50 years.

It may seem rather presumptuous to attempt to concisely articulate when and why the counseling wars came to exist. For anyone who has endeavored to study the history of the conflict, it is apparent that it is more of a theological debate than a debate over best practices in counseling. In fact, one could argue the skill of counseling is just a landscape, a context so to speak, where theologians have chosen to pitch their tent in order to argue different disciplines within systematic theology. This is not meant to imply that an understanding of theology is not essential to a counseling process that best represents the teaching of Scripture. However, it would be wise to recognize that much of the debate and conflict revolves around proof texting and a propositional theology emphasis rather than meaningful discussions that are true to a contextual reading of Scripture.[24]

To narrow the discussion to counseling that flows from a Christian worldview does little to avoid the conflict. Nevertheless, in the current theological-academic-psychological landscape, there are recognized leaders within the Christian faith who do an excellent job of articulating different approaches to counseling from a Christian worldview. While this does not mean these spokesmen speak on behalf of all counselors, identifying them and understanding the different

---

[24] Vanhoozer has discussed the reality of propositional theology in the context of the modern church is his book, *The Drama of Doctrine, a Canonical Linguistic Approach to Christian Theology*, 2005.

approaches to counseling does provide a launching point from which one can at least organize the discussion.

It is helpful to begin with at least a summary definition of how counseling is defined by those who do not hold a Christian worldview. This does not necessarily mean these definitions are completely mutually exclusive from a Christian worldview, but it is apparent that these definitions do not invoke concepts and ideas rooted in Scripture. The American Counseling Association defines counseling as "a professional relationship that empowers diverse individuals, families, and groups to accomplish mental health, wellness, education, and career goals."[25] This definition provides an accurate representation of how the skill of counseling is understood in a contemporary context, speaking to the formality and professionalism of the relationship and emphasizing health and wellness, with particular emphasis on mental health that results in specific life goals.

In 2000, Eric Johnson, former professor of Pastoral Care at Southern Baptist Theological Seminary in Louisville, served as an editor for the book entitled, *Psychology and Christianity, Five Views.* Johnson argued that during the 1970s, serious concerns began to be raised about the perceived dangers of accommodating the Christian tradition to that of modern psychology – and thus initiated the five positions contained in the book.[26]

The five positions consist of the *Levels-of-Explanation* view, presented by David G. Myers, the *Integration* view, presented by Stanton L. Jones, the *Christian Psychology* view, presented by Robert C. Roberts and P. J. Watson, the *Transformational Psychology* view, presented by John H. Coe and Todd W. Hall, and finally the *Biblical Counseling* view, presented by

---

[25] https://www.counseling.org/about-us/about-aca/20-20-a-vision-for-the-future-of-counseling/consensus-definition-of-counseling, February 11, 2020.

[26] Eric L. Johnson and David G. Myers, eds., Psychology and Christianity: Five Views, 2nd ed. (Downers Grove, Ill.: IVP Academic, 2010), 31.

David Powlison. Since 2000, and even in the second edition in 2010, the five positions contained in the book have morphed into different positions, assimilated into larger schools of thought, and some have become less popular or more popular, all resulting in a different landscape within the evangelical church and associated academic institutions. What has stayed consistent within the conversation is a tension between what is described as a *Biblical Counseling* view and other counseling views that also hold a Christian worldview. At the same time, a more adversarial tension exists between what is described as "Biblical counseling" with what is best understood as secular counseling. One cannot understand the complexities of these tensions without an understanding of how the Biblical Counseling movement developed in the last 50 years.

It should be noted that the use of the word *Biblical* to describe the *Biblical Counseling* view is problematic as it hinges on what is intended or understood by the use of the adjective "Biblical." This should not come as a surprise, for the word *Biblical*, when used as an adjective, adds little clarity to meaningful conversations that seek to arrive at understanding. To avoid this problem, it is best to refer to this view as *Nouthetic Counseling*, the name chosen by its founder, Jay Adams. The word *nouthetic* comes from the Greek word *nouthetein* (νουθετεῖν.), and can be defined as the action of admonishing, warning, counseling, or exhorting. Paul uses the word in Romans 15:14 to argue that believers who are full of knowledge and goodness are able to counsel one another.

When Jay Adams wrote *Competent to Counsel* in 1970, he struck a nerve and created a movement. At the same time, he galvanized an opposition by asserting that psychotherapeutic professions were a false pastorate, interlopers on tasks that properly belonged to pastors.[27] David Powlison thoroughly documents the history and development of the

---

[27] David Powlison, *The Biblical Counseling Movement* (Greensboro: New Growth Press, 2010), XVII.

Nouthetic Counseling movement in his book, *The Biblical Counseling Movement* (2010). Heath Lambert articulated the theology of the view in *A Theology of Biblical Counseling* (2016). Lambert's book is important as it has become somewhat of a doctrinal statement for the position held by many faculty members at Southern Baptist Seminaries. While impossible to concisely summarize the development of such a significant movement as the Nouthetic Counseling view, an overview of the development of the movement is helpful.

Two movements came to full fruition in the 1970s that led to the development of the Nouthetic Counseling movement. The first movement could be labeled as Fundamentalism. Fundamentalism emerged as a response to a shift in how the academic world approached and accepted the Bible. Christianity was undergoing an intellectual crisis in the nineteenth century sparked partially by Darwin's *Origin of the Species*, which was published in 1859, and the development of German higher criticism of the Bible. The Princeton theologians famously addressed the issue of Biblical authority in works such as *Inspiration and Authority of the Bible* by B. B. Warfield. Between the years 1910-1915, *The Fundamentals*, a collection of nine essays were written. *The Fundamentals* were a statement of the fundamentals of Christianity meant to refute the voices that were questioning the authority and accuracy of Scripture.[28]

The fundamentalist movement in America contended with "modernist" views of the Bible by applying an approach of rigid Biblical emphasis to matters of faith and science. Fundamentalism grew out of the Second Great Awakening and eventually created a populist outlook focused on conversions that also introduced an anti-intellectual strain into evangelicalism.[29] The anti-intellectual strain of fundamentalism does not

---

[28] Heath Lambert, *The Biblical Counseling Movement After Adams* (Heath Lambert, 2012), 200.

[29] Frances Fitzgerald, *The Evangelicals: The Struggle to Shape America* (Simon & Schuster, 2017), 3.

imply that the leaders were not intelligent, nor should one infer that the movement was not committed to learning and study. Rather, the term "anti-intellectual" refers to the movement's withdrawal from established academic institutions and the creation of its own Bible institutes. There were 50 such Bible institutes in 1930, but by 1950 the number had increased to 144.[30] Many of these new Bible institutes would eventually embrace counseling philosophies deemphasizing the importance of psychology, psychotherapy, psychiatry, etc.

The second movement that heavily influenced the Nouthetic Counseling view is the new-Calvinism surge of the last 40 years.[31] Presbyterian Pastor Jay Adams represents the second movement that came to fruition in the 1970s. The perception of many within the Nouthetic Counseling movement is that the church had neglected a robustly *Biblical* approach to counseling for more than a century, dating from the time of the Puritans until Jay Adams wrote *Competent to Counsel* in 1970.[32]

Adams was largely influenced by reformed theologian and Christian apologist Cornelius Van Til, who taught at Westminster Theological Seminary. Eventually Adams would pass the mantle to a second generation of Nouthetic Counselors. Many would consider Powlison an intellectual leader of the Nouthetic Counseling approach. He would follow in the Reformed tradition of both his mentor Jay Adams and Cornelius Van Til. "Since the mid-1960s, when Presbyterian pastor Jay Adams first laid out its principles, Nouthetic Counseling has become dominant in conservative Christian denominations that follow Reformed

---

[30] Frances Fitzgerald, *The Evangelicals: The Struggle to Shape America* (Simon & Schuster, 2017), 148.

[31] Time magazine published an article March 12, 2009, listing Calvinism as one of the 10 ideas changing the world right now.

[32] Heath Lambert, *The Biblical Counseling Movement After Adams* (Heath Lambert, 2012), 25-26.

(or Calvinist) theology."[33] Powlison suggested that Jay Adams taught, "The Bible, as interpreted by Reformed Protestants, taught pastors the matters necessary to counsel competently."[34]

With the growing influence of Calvinism over the past 40 years among evangelical seminaries and churches, an increased emphasis on Nouthetic Counseling has also taken place. Jay Adams' seminal work, *Competent to Counsel*, has become a standard-bearer for those who hold to a Nouthetic Counseling model that asserts the Bible (through the lens of Reformed theology) is sufficient as the only necessary resource for counseling.

One of the significant attributes of the movement has been its ability to unify different traditions of faith behind a common approach to counseling. For instance, premillennialists and amillennialists, dispensationalists and covenant theologians, Reformed and Lutheran, have embraced this common counseling ideology even when their traditions of faith disagree on matters of foundational hermeneutics, soteriology, and eschatology. So, what is this unifying principle that is so compelling to unify different traditions of faith? It is a passion and conviction regarding the perceived role of Scripture in counseling, and probably more importantly, the actual role of any other source of wisdom in counseling.

On the surface, this unifying principle, the perceived role of Scripture in counseling, seems rather innocuous to those who hold a high view of Scripture. However, within the Nouthetic Counseling view, the emphasis on Scripture results in a leap to a use of the adjective "Biblical." The phrase Biblical Counseling has become somewhat synonymous with

---

[33] Eric L. Johnson and David G1 Myers, eds., Psychology and Christianity: Five Views, 2nd ed. (IVP Academic, 2010), 276.

[34] David Powilson, *The Biblical Counseling Movement* (New Growth Press, 2010), XVII.

Nouthetic Counseling. Lambert posits that Nouthetic Counseling and Biblical Counseling are two sides of the same coin.[35]

The Nouthetic Counseling movement's use of the term *Biblical* demonstrates the movement's tension, sometimes conflict, with other Christian approaches. David Powlison observes, "Our differences turn on how we actually understand and work out Scripture's appropriate place of authority."[36] Powlison is correct. How does one understand the authority of Scripture? But this question has further implications. How does one understand the role and place of other sources of wisdom in regard to counseling? Herein is the crux of the matter.

To be clear, there is nothing essentially wrong with the question, "What is Biblical Counseling?" But within the conversation regarding counseling from a Christian worldview perspective, the question can be unhelpful. Too often the conversations deteriorate into posturing, creating strawmen, speaking past one another, false caricatures, etc. To state it directly, the conversation turns into a debate about who *really* believes the Bible or who believes the Bible *more*. This is unfortunate, for in many circles those who are discussing different views on counseling both aspire to a high view of Scripture.

For example, the Association of Biblical Counselors defines Biblical Counseling as, "a fluid event and process of a Spirit-empowered Christ follower providing face-to-face ministry of the Word to others."[37] There is a lot to like about this definition. However, the adjective "Biblical" and the phrase "ministry of the Word" are pregnant with subtle innuendoes, insinuations, and presuppositions.

---

[35] https://www.thegospelcoalition.org/article/two-sides-of-the-counseling-coin, February 14, 2020.
[36] Eric L. Johnson et al., *Psychology and Christianity*, 2nd ed. (Downers Grove: IVP Academic, 2010), under "1677," Electronic Format.
[37] https://christiancounseling.com/blog/definition-biblical-counseling. February 14, 2020.

To be fair, if one delves into the abundance of writing from those who hold to a Nouthetic Counseling approach, one would find that the movement has grown and changed to such an extent that much of the time common ground can be found between Nouthetic Counselors and other Christian counselors. Sometimes one has to strain to find true differences. This is especially true in how medicine, psychology, and general revelation are viewed. Yet still, the question that is usually posed is, "What is Biblical Counseling?" This implies that other views are not "Biblical," or perhaps better stated, "as Biblical."

The purpose of the use of the adjective "Biblical" in regard to counseling is easily understood in an evangelical context. What conservative evangelical university or seminary would advertise a *Masters of Arts in Nonbiblical Counseling*? Yet, if that same university or seminary were to simply advertise a *Master of Arts in Counseling*, omitting the adjective "Biblical," some (and it could be argued many) would read it as *Master of Arts in Nonbiblical Counseling*. This is the conundrum. How can one argue that they take the Bible seriously in the context of counseling and not use the word "Biblical?" Regardless, when discussing counseling there are better questions to ask than, "What is Biblical Counseling?" One might ask, "What model of counseling best represents the whole teaching of Scripture?" Still another question could be, "What model of counseling is congruent with Scripture?" Still better yet, "Where can wisdom be found?" While the differences between these questions might seem insignificant, the questions do provide a pathway to an honest discussion.

So where can wisdom be found? Scripture! Paul tells Timothy that the Scripture is able to make him *wise* unto salvation.[38] While some might dispute the dating of the canonization of the Old Testament and the access Timothy might have had to a complete Old Testament, there is no denying that Timothy knew the Scriptures and that in them wisdom could

---

[38] 2 Timothy 3:15.

be found. Paul further elaborates about the profitability of the Scripture to Timothy's life and Scripture's ability to fully equip Timothy to every good work.[39]

If one is going to get wisdom, one must search the Scriptures. If one is to counsel another to become wise, get wisdom, be wise, one must guide them with Scripture. The preeminence, centrality, and authority of Scripture is essential to finding wisdom. Any counseling model that seeks to find wisdom without a proper perspective concerning Scripture will miss the mark.

Where else can wisdom be found? Just asking this question can result in an unnecessary debate between those who hold different views on counseling while also holding a high view of Scripture. This is most unfortunate. Those who believe that God's wisdom can be found in God's revelation outside of Scripture can be accused of not believing in the sufficiency of Scripture. Once again, just as the adjective *Biblical* must be defined by both the speaker and the hearer, the concept of the sufficiency of Scripture must be further defined. A better phrase might be *the sufficiency of revelation, God's revelation.*

At issue is how Scripture interacts with other revelation. In regard to counseling, how does Scripture interact with other disciplines? Both the Protestant and Evangelical tradition of faith hold to the five *solas* of the Reformation. *Sola Scriptura* is perhaps the most challenging of the *solas* to retrieve.[40] The goal of counseling, to find wisdom, is best understood when one correctly ascertains the concept of *Sola Scriptura.* Understanding

---

[39] 2 Timothy 3:15-17. The use of the word ἐξηρτισμένος in 2 Timothy 3:15-17 speaks to Paul's emphasis on the importance of Scripture in the sanctification process of the believer. Along with 2 Peter 1:3, these passage are also often used to express the doctrine of the sufficiency of Scripture. However, one must determine what is meant by *sufficiency* of Scripture and one must still investigate the relation of Scripture to other sources of wisdom.

[40] Kevin J. Vanhoozer, *Biblical Authority After Babel: Retrieving the Solas in the Spirit of Mere Protestant Christianity* (Grand Rapids: Brazos Press, 2016), under "3123," Electronic Format.

the correct meaning of *Sola Scriptura* answers other important questions. In what sense is Scripture authoritative? How does Scripture integrate with other disciplines such as psychology, psychotherapy, philosophy, sociology, anthropology, medicine, science, etc.? Can God's wisdom be found in these disciplines?

At issue is an understanding that *Sola Scriptura* does not exclude extrabiblical sources of wisdom. In other words, *Sola Scriptura* does not refer to *Scripture in isolation,* but rather *Scripture alone as authoritative.* The context of the Reformation was an understanding that Scripture not be taken captive by Roman Catholic tradition.[41] At its core, much of the Reformation blossomed out of an dispute between Martin Luther and the Roman Catholic Church regarding the role of tradition and church authority in contrast to the authority of Scripture.

Sola Scriptura would not have been understood to rule out all other sources of wisdom, but rather would have been understood to acknowledge the authority of Scripture over all other sources. The counselor must consequently begin with Scripture because Scripture declares itself to be authoritative and is self-interpreting, and the counselor must assess wisdom from any other source solely on the basis and authority of Scripture.

So why should the counselor and counselee search for additional wisdom not found in Scripture? *Sola Scriptura* recognizes that Scripture is authoritative over other sources of knowledge, but instead of prohibiting discovery from other sources, Scripture actually encourages the seeking of knowledge through other sources. Scripture correctly understood and applied helps us to understand, organize, and learn from other sources.

It is one thing to argue the evidence for finding wisdom outside of Scripture, from the context of Martin Luther arguing against the tradition of the Catholic Church in the administration of indulgences. It

---

[41] Ibid., under "3253," Electronic Format.

is another thing altogether to argue that Scripture itself encourages the counselor and counselee to learn from other sciences. Science can be understood as the observation and documentation of the factual qualities of the natural world and the development and testing of theories that coordinate and explain these facts.[42] Scripture states that the natural world does have something to say about God. In Psalm 19, the author states that the natural world continually declares the glory of God and proclaims the work of God's hand throughout all the earth. Alongside the natural revelation is God's revelation through Scripture contained in Psalm 19:7-11. God's wisdom is evident to the Psalmist by means of the natural world, and that is appraised through what is revealed in Scripture. Paul argues that observable creation is sufficient to reveal invisible things about God, including his divine nature and eternal power.[43] The fact that God revealed through the natural world to demonstrate His existence and attributes exposes wisdom in the sciences in ways that educate counselors on how they can seek wisdom for themselves and others.

Scripture includes the writings of those who have learned through observation. Qoheleth (or Solomon), the author of Ecclesiastes, states that he has learned through observation.[44] Through observation Qoheleth provides conclusions and counsel that are intended to guide the reader to make the most of his or her life on this earth under the sun.[45] Qoheleth states that he sees predictability to life, although it is not without exception.[46] He has observed what brings wellness to individuals and what patterns of behavior diminish wellness.[47]

---

[42] Eric L. Johnson et al., *Psychology and Christianity*, 2nd ed. (IVP Academic, 2010), under "1227," Electronic Format.
[43] Romans 1:20.
[44] Ecclesiastes 1:12-14.
[45] 8:15.
[46] 9:11.
[47] 1:12-18.

Solomon, writing Proverbs, uses pithy statements to convey truths he has learned from observation. Rather than simply passing on what he has learned, the author actually challenges the hearer to consider certain things in the natural world and learn from them.[48] Christ also admonished his followers to consider things in the natural world through observation and learn principles for well-living.[49] Christ continually illustrated in His teachings a mastery of the Scripture, the natural world, and the nature of man.

Counseling that strives to get wisdom seeks to learn from the observations made in various disciplines and then to organize and filter these observations through the authority of Scripture in order to bring wisdom to individuals and communities. It is understood that from a secular standpoint sciences or disciplines can stray from the special revelation of Scripture. However, to ignore the knowledge these sciences and disciplines bring is antithetical to the teaching of Scripture itself. God has chosen to limit His actions and speech, but at the same time, He has created humans as rational beings capable of learning more about the reality around them through the exercise of reason and curiosity.[50]

Does Scripture actually *encourage* one to *get wisdom* outside of Scripture? This question has been central to much deliberation between counseling models that aspire to a high view of Scripture. In 1991, John Coe, proponent of Transformational Psychology, published an article entitled, "Why Biblical Counseling is Unbiblical."[51] The title of his article is clever in that he asserts that those who advocate for Biblical Counseling are actually violating Scripture. The article centers around an exposition of Proverbs 24:30-34. Coe argues that the writer observed something,

---

[48] Proverbs 6:6-8.
[49] Luke 12:27-40.
[50] Eric L. Johnson et al., *Psychology and Christianity*, 2nd ed. (IVP Academic, 2010), under "1270," Electronic Format.
[51] John Coe., Evangelical Theological Society papers, ETS-0130, 1991.

applied his heart to it, and then learned a lesson and gained wisdom. Coe concludes that wisdom can be found outside of Scripture.

A rebuttal to Coe's argument is written by a proponent of a Biblical Counseling view.[52] The author, Kyle Johnston, argues that Coe has incorrectly deduced that wisdom can be found outside of propositional theology. Johnston argues that mere observation of events in this world is not a strong epistemological foundation. He asserts that the text Coe used in Proverbs does not indicate that wisdom can come from a person's observation of the structure of the cosmos.

To be fair, it is questionable to believe the author of Proverbs intended for his primary audience to find a *par excellence* dogma on common grace, general revelation, and natural revelation when he told the story of a man observing a garden. When observations of the behavior of ants (Proverbs 6) are one's foundational theological framework to argue for the merits of psychotherapy and medical assistance for neurological chemical imbalances, it is reasonable to reevaluate one's hermeneutical approach to Scripture.

But at the same time, it seems presumptuous to argue that observation does not lead to wisdom from God because *technically speaking* the world does not contain God's wisdom, it was only created by wisdom as is stated in Proverbs 3:19-20. Furthermore, eventually both sides of these arguments reduce themselves to arguing over degrees of the use of Scripture and projected logical fallacies of slippery slope arguments. This is reflected in Johnston's acknowledgement concerning a "biblical counselor's" use of science:

---

[52] Kyle Johnston, Are Biblical Counselors Unbiblical: Evaluating Transformational Psychology's Exegetical Foundation, https://s3-us-west-2.amaxonaws.com/acbcdigitalresources/resources/ACBC+ESSAUS/2017/Are+Biblical+Counselors+Unbiblical+Kyle+Johnson.pdf. Downloaded February 15, 2020.

However, it is worth emphasizing that, even though biblical counselors rely on the Scriptures in counseling, the biblical counseling approach is not at all opposed to scientific investigation. As we saw when considering Proverbs 24:30-34, the sage keenly observes and reflects upon what he sees—he keeps his eyes open, and we should, too! Biblical counselors can learn from sources other than Scripture, because numerous sources (from scientific research to literature, and more) contribute toward our knowledge of people. And academic developments in a variety of disciplines will always be of interest to those who practice biblical counseling—although the biblical approach to how that knowledge is viewed and used would be different from the TP model. The TP model may overly exalt such knowledge, considering it to be a non-propositional source of wisdom. The Transformational Psychologist is potentially in danger of calling human knowledge God's wisdom. In contrast, the biblical counseling model recognizes academic developments positively—yet views them as potentially helpful sources of knowledge, rather than as new authoritative moral truths. Advances in knowledge can be helpful and enthusiastically welcomed, but a thoughtful biblical counselor would not equate those academic advances with God's wisdom.[53]

So while arguing that observation does not produce godly wisdom, Johnston does state:

1. Numerous sources, from scientific research to literature and more, contribute toward our knowledge of people.

---

[53] Ibid.

2. Academic development in a variety of disciplines will always be of interest to those who practice biblical counseling.
3. The TP model *may* (emphasis added) overly exalt such knowledge, considering it to be a non-propositional source of wisdom.
4. The TP model is *potentially* (emphasis added) in danger of calling human knowledge God's wisdom.[54]

The point here is not to criticize either Coe or Johnston. However, this exchange is a prime example of how the debate has been conducted since 1979, and is oftentimes still conducted today. Johnston equates Coe's use of observation as an attempt to equate science with Scripture. Coe equates the observation of a sloth's field with observations made in psychology, psychotherapy, and possibly psychiatry. Johnston states that one can learn from science, observation, and gain knowledge from academia, as long as one doesn't call it wisdom. Coe argues that there is such a thing as an over-reliance on Scripture. Johnston argues for a possible overreliance on knowledge gained from observation. Neither discusses the complexity of the fact that much of the encouragement to gain wisdom by observing commands in the book of Proverbs are commands to observe the saying of one's parents. Are the parents reciting the Torah? What if one's parents are not wise?

The point is that this type of exposition misses the clear and intended purpose of Scripture. Both sides unintentionally create false mutually exclusive dichotomies. Both sides unintentionally teach specific theological concepts using passages in ways that would be foreign to the author's original intent. And both sides often mischaracterize the opposing view by implying one might use the Scripture too much or not

---

[54] Ibid.

enough. It seems the author of Proverbs loved wisdom that was gleaned by special revelation (God's Word), and at the same time was wise enough to observe the world around him and use that wisdom to help people. Furthermore, he was wiser still to understand that these skills were not competing or mutually exclusive. "The authors of Proverbs drew inspiration through keen observations and cogent reflections on creation, but they brought to their task Israel's world-and-life view and used creation to confirm it."[55]

However, even when one realizes there are other sources for wisdom, one must ask another question in the context of counseling. Is there an inherent danger using other disciplines, such as psychology, psychotherapy, and psychiatry? Possibly.

A great deal of contemporary content within psychology, psychotherapy, and psychiatry has originated from a secular-humanistic worldview. The view is generally held by secularists that psychology began with the ancient Greeks. It is often believed in these contexts that psychology is a relatively new field of study compared to other scientific disciplines. Furthermore, its initial development is as recent as the 1870s in Europe with Wilhelm Wundt and in North America with the writings of William James.[56]

Any intentional reading of the origins of psychology will reveal that a secular worldview has influenced a lot of psychological presuppositions and approaches. Treating poor decisions as a disease can further discredit psychology, psychotherapy, and psychiatry when compared with how Scripture discusses human responsibility and accountability.

---

[55] Bruce K. Waltke, *The Book of Proverbs: Chapters 1-15* (Eerdmans, 2004), 82.

[56] Mark A. Yarhouse and James N. Sells, *Family Therapies a Comprehensive Christian Appraisal* (InterVarsity Press, 2008), 45.

However, properly understood, psychology is the study of the psyche or, perhaps better stated, the study of the soul (*logia psuche*),[57] and the study of the soul has been going on for as long as humans have been around. Psychotherapy has been called the profession of soul healing.[58] This means that the idea that psychology, the study of the soul, began in the last 200 years is not accurate. Humans are relational, and there is an intrinsic need to make relationships work. It is true that the ideas of Greek philosophers and modern psychology are more recent. However, Old Testament authors, predating Greek philosophers, were discussing the concept of soul wellness over 1,500 years prior to the writings of Plato, Aristotle, and Epicurus.[59] The goal of seeking wisdom to make the soul well has been an overriding theme of the Scriptures since the problem of sin entered the world in Genesis.

This need to find wisdom exceeds the idea merely to survive, expanding to issues of self-consciousness and self-awareness regarding how we are included and belong in community. When one begins with a Biblical worldview regarding community, one finds there have always been those who observe, learn, and create systems of treatment to help others, and that help transcends culture, circumstances, and time.[60] The reality is the disciplines that lead to helping relationships, which includes one's relationship with oneself, has a tradition spanning millennia.[61]

It is noteworthy that the idea of healing, which is associated with wellness, and the concept of soul, which can be understood to refer to the

---

[57] A thoroughgoing psychology understood in light of the authority of Scripture is the inquiry pertaining to the human person, involving both material and immaterial aspects.

[58] Mark A. Yarhouse and James N. Sells, *Family Therapies, A Comprehensive Christian Appraisal* (InterVarsity Press, 2008), 39.

[59] Eric L. Johnson et al., *Psychology and Christianity*, 2nd ed. (IVP Academic, 2010), under "84," Electronic Format.

[60] Mark A. Yarhouse and James N. Sells, Family Therapies a Comprehensive Christian Appraisal (InterVarsity Press, 2008), 16.

[61] Ibid., 46.

entirety of a person – mental relational, emotional, etc. – are both conveyed in the non-religious understanding of psychological counseling.

Psychology, as a self-conscious field of experimental study, is argued to have begun as a proper science in 1879 when Wilhelm Wundt founded his laboratory in Leipzig, Germany. The first sophisticated psychologies in the West were developed by Greek philosopher-therapists and attempted to describe human nature, including its fundamental ills which impede wellness, on the basis of experience and rigorous reflection in light of prior thought.[62]

Based on observation, human beings have learned over time there are evidenced-based methods that really help people in their personal relationships.[63] With time and testing, these observations are formed into "best practices" – the idea that certain practices yield the best results with most people. So while the Christian counselor must be mindful of worldly wisdom that does not align with Scripture, the Christian counselor can embrace the blessing of reason, the gift of observation, the value of experiencing a life that is a gift from God, and glean godly wisdom from other disciplines that can be organized into best practices to assist him or her in guiding others to *get wisdom.*

And how do these "best practices" from other disciplines align with Scripture? The reality is the sovereignty of God over all existence, as revealed in the Bible, determines what is true about practices toward all of reality and toward academic subject matter in particular.[64] Solomon argues that observation does bring about knowledge.[65] But the wisdom

---

[62] Rorbert I. Watson and Rand B. Evans, *The Great Psychologist: A History of Psychological Thought*, 5th ed. (Harper Collins, 1991), 11-12.

[63] Stanley B. Baker, "A New View of Evidence-Based Practice," Counseling Today, December 1, 2012, https://ct.counseling.org/2012/12/a-new-view-of-evidence-based-practice/.

[64] Eric L. Johnson and David G1 Myers, eds., Psychology and Christianity: Five Views, 2nd ed. (IVP Academic, 2010), 102.

[65] The author of Ecclesiastes and Proverbs writes as a scientist, making observations and recording the best practices by which young people should live their lives. Although

gleaned through disciplines such as psychology, psychotherapy, and psychiatry and verified through testing and research, when seen through a Biblical worldview can provide valuable tools to guide others. And those who wish to guide others to *get wisdom* must continually be asking, "Where can wisdom be found?"

---

these writings are Special Revelation ergo they are in the Bible, they still teach the value of observing, learning, reasoning, and applying.

4

Foundations of Science

Jeffrey R. Christianson, Ph.D

INTRODUCTION

Since science is foundational to the discipline of psychology,[1] it is necessary to examine the foundations of science. The field of science is extremely broad in scope, encompassing many varied disciplines, but it is unified in its general methodology and goals. Mirriam-Webster defines the field of science as "knowledge or a system of knowledge covering general truths or the operation of general laws especially as obtained and tested through the scientific method".[2] Along similar lines, the Science Council states that "Science is the pursuit and application of knowledge and understanding of the natural and social world following a systematic methodology based on evidence."[3] As seen from both of these definitions, the many diverse disciplines within the field of science are united by a systematic, evidenced-based methodology whose goals are to generalize and apply knowledge.

---

[1] See chapter "Psychology: Discipline or Philosophy?".

[2] https://www.merriam-webster.com/dictionary/science, accessed 12/1/2020.

[3] https://sciencecouncil.org/about-science/our-definition-of-science/, accessed 12/1/2020.

To examine the foundations of science, then, is to examine the basis of its methodology and goals. The systematic, evidenced-based methodology of science is not reliable unless reality allows for systematization and consistent experiences. Similarly, the goals of science to generalize and apply knowledge are only achievable to the extent that, in reality, there is a correspondence between human reasoning and the workings of nature (which must themselves be consistent). Furthermore, the goals of science are not ultimate in and of themselves. The drive to generalize and apply knowledge assumes both an ultimate purpose to reality and that it is in alignment with an ultimate ethic. It is clear that metaphysical (especially ontological and teleological), epistemological, and ethical assumptions are foundational to science.

Prior to examining these foundations, however, it must be recognized that the plainly-interpreted, authoritative revelation of the Creator is the only firmly-grounded epistemological starting point for any worldview analysis.[4] In terms of the current analysis, this means that the metaphysical, epistemological, and ethical assumptions of science, if they are accurate, are derivative of the Creator and revealed authoritatively in Scripture. Therefore, science can only be properly examined from the Biblical worldview.

As such, this chapter addresses the sufficiency of Scripture to ground science and, as a result, the scientific discipline of psychology in the Biblical worldview. Science in general is examined in terms of metaphysics, epistemology, and ethics, and then implications for psychology in particular are specified.

---

[4] See chapter "General Distinctiveness of This Approach: Psychology and Counseling as Disciplines Born from the Biblical Worldview."

SCIENCE AND METAPHYSICS

Metaphysics is naturally rooted in origins, and the Biblical doctrines most closely associated with the events of creation (the origin of the physical universe) and the fall (the origin of evil in the physical universe) are the same doctrines that ground Biblical metaphysics – namely, the doctrines of God, Man, Nature, and the relationship that each of these has with evil.[5] Therefore, it is necessary to examine the dependence of science on the Creator-creation distinction, the man-nature distinction, and the effects of the fall.

By the Creator-creation distinction we mean that God, as Creator, is categorically distinct from His creation. This is demonstrated by His independence from creation (aseity),[6] His existence outside of time (eternality)[7] and space (omnipresence),[8] His ultimate sovereignty over all of creation,[9] His infinite knowledge of all creation (omniscience),[10] and even creation itself.[11] This distinction has a number of implications for science. First, as wholly dependent on the creation, science cannot directly study God. While creation is certainly revelatory of the Creator,[12] God Himself cannot be subjected to the experimentation demanded by the scientific method. His interaction with creation is founded upon accomplishing His purpose[13] according to His unsearchable wisdom and ways,[14] which are only partially revealed to us by His Word, not by any of

[5] The relationships between historical events and doctrine as they are both revealed in Scripture, including those discussed here, have been greatly expounded in the Bible Framework course (https://bibleframework.com) by Charles A. Clough.
[6] Genesis 1:1; John 1:1-3; Hebrews 1:2; Revelation 4:11.
[7] Psalm 90:2; Isaiah 44:6; John 8:58.
[8] 1 Kings 8:27; Psalm 139:7-12.
[9] Isaiah 46:8-13, 55:11.
[10] Psalm 147:5; Hebrews 4:13.
[11] Romans 1:20.
[12] Ibid.; Psalm 19:11-4.
[13] Isaiah 46:10, 55:11.
[14] Isaiah 40:13; Rom. 11:33-35.

our own experimentation. Second, the Creator designed and authoritatively guarantees systematization and consistency within creation. God's very act of creating was completed systematically[15] and resulted in stable (namable) categories.[16] Furthermore, He actively sustains all of creation[17] in an age where He has explicitly promised a consistency within nature.[18] As noted above, this systematization and consistency is foundational (even presuppositional) to the evidence-based methodology of science. Third, the Creator's transcendence above His creation is the basis for the fact that the ultimate purpose of all of creation is to display the glory of God. The doxological purpose of all things is evident throughout all of Scripture,[19] including in (but not limited to) the act of creation,[20] all of nature,[21] man's activity,[22] man's redemption,[23] and God's interaction with man.[24] Thus, as the ultimate purpose of all things, the reflection of the glory of God is the basis for the goals of science. In particular, the scientific generalization of knowledge is the detailed study of God's creating and sustaining work, effectively lending an ever more attentive ear to nature's declaration of the glory of God.

Science is also based on the man-nature distinction within the creation. Scripture is clear that man is an utterly unique part of creation. In contrast with the rest of nature, man bears the image of God,[25] was created male and female from one body,[26] was originally tasked with

---

[15] Genesis 1 details the systematic forming and filling of the formless and void.

[16] Genesis 1:5, 1:8, 1:10, 2:19-20.

[17] Colossians 1:17; Hebrews 1:3.

[18] Genesis 8:22, 9:11.

[19] Cone, Christopher, *Redacted Dominionism: A Biblical Approach to Grounding Environmental Responsibility* (Wipf & Stock, 2012), 91-92.

[20] Revelation 4:11.

[21] Psalm 19.

[22] 1 Corinthians 10:31; 1 Peter 4:11.

[23] Ephesians 1:5-12.

[24] Isaiah 60:21; Isaiah 61:3; Ephesians 3.

[25] Genesis 1:26-27.

[26] Genesis 2:21-22.

dominion over nature,[27] is responsible for making moral choices,[28] is inherently aware of God's moral standard,[29] is capable of love,[30] and has capacity for a complex level of knowledge and reasoning.[31] There are at least two major implications of this distinction for science. First, the man-nature distinction is the basis for the primary sub-classification of scientific disciplines. Natural sciences explore systems in which the behavior of nature is the primary subject, whereas social sciences explore systems in which human behavior is the primary subject. This will be explored further later on; for now, it is sufficient to note that the uniqueness and complexity of man must inevitably lead to significant differences in the methodologies of natural and social sciences. Second, the man-nature distinction indicates that man, and man alone in the natural world, is capable of exploring science. The Creator's command to man to exercise responsible dominion over nature implies that He created man with the capacity to generalize and apply knowledge of nature based on careful observation of it. Indeed, this is what Adam did when God brought land animals and birds to him for naming,[32] which implies a generalized understanding of function and purpose.[33] Application of this knowledge certainly would have been necessary to "have dominion over the birds of the air, and over the cattle, over all the earth, and over every creeping thing that creeps on the earth."[34] That we must say "*would have been* necessary", however, acknowledges a third major aspect to the metaphysical foundations of science.

---

[27] Genesis 1:28-29.
[28] Genesis 2:16-17.
[29] Romans 1:20, 2:14-15.
[30] Genesis 2:18, 23-25, 22:2; Deuteronomy 6:5 (cf. Matthew 22:37-39).
[31] *e.g.*, Luke 1:1-4; Ephesians 1:17-18ff.
[32] Genesis 2:19-20.
[33] Genesis 1:3-4, 7-8, 9-10.
[34] Genesis 1:26.

Not only is science based on distinctions inherent in the created order, but science as we know it is catastrophically affected by the fallen state of the world. The fall of man resulted in his physical[35] and spiritual[36] death, his naturally rebellious and defiant disposition toward God,[37] the corruption of his knowledge by falsehood, lies, and deceit,[38] and even the qualitative changes to nature that brought about its inefficiencies[39] and overall bondage to corruption.[40] These effects have multiple colossal implications for science. First, man is incapable of perfectly exploring science. Both random and systematic errors are commonplace in even the most carefully constructed scientific experiments and measurements. While these errors can sometimes be minimized, bounded, and/or approximated, the fact remains that human error plays a large role in limiting scientific methodology, efficiency, and knowledge. Second, man is capable of using science as a tool of rebellion. Whether it is, for example, an individual scientist who fabricates data for personal gain or an entire society of scientists that disguises philosophical presuppositions as scientific knowledge, the result is that scientific claims cannot be taken at face value. They must be critically examined by both internal scientific processes and an accurate (*i.e.*, Biblical) external worldview. Third, science investigates a broken and abnormal state of nature and human behavior. Therefore, the knowledge of nature or human behavior that is observed or discovered is qualitatively different from that which would be observed or discovered in a similar study in the perfect original creation or in the perfectly remade creation yet to come.

---

[35] Genesis 2:17, 3:19.

[36] Genesis 3:9-10; Ephesians 2:1-3.

[37] Romans 1:21-23, 3:10-18.

[38] Genesis 3:6, 13; Isaiah 5:20; 2 Corinthians 11:3-4; Colossians 2:8; 1 Timothy 6:20.

[39] Genesis 3:17-19.

[40] Romans 8:20-22.

SCIENCE AND EPISTEMOLOGY

Since science is largely defined by its methodology for pursuing knowledge, in some senses it *is* an epistemological approach to knowledge. However, it emphatically is *not* a foundational epistemological approach sufficient to ground metaphysical truth, which is only the case for the authoritative revelation of the Creator. Rather, the epistemological approach of science is *derived* from metaphysical truth. Scientific methodology is now examined more closely and its metaphysical grounding and inherent limitations are identified.

At its core, the scientific method is a carefully-controlled interplay between inductive (or empirical or *a posteriori*) and deductive (or rational or *a priori*) thought. Mirriam-Webster defines the scientific method as "principles and procedures for the systematic pursuit of knowledge involving the recognition and formulation of a problem, the collection of data through observation and experiment, and the formulation and testing of hypotheses."[41] There are numerous variations of this definition that specify any number of specific steps, but in the end they all boil down to this general pattern:

1. Investigate and define a problem (induction)
2. Hypothesize some general, underlying phenomena or principles and what observable behavior would or would not follow if the hypothesis is true (deduction)
3. Construct and complete an experiment that has the capability of falsifying the hypothesis (induction)
4. Add the result to the investigative data and repeat

---

[41] https://www.merriam-webster.com/dictionary/scientific%20method, accessed 12/1/2020.

Step 2 is where generalization of scientific knowledge originates. The hypothesized underlying phenomena or principles often apply more generally than just to the specified problem and are not directly observable. They serve as a model of unseen reality. Therefore, the hypothesis cannot be proven true by induction; some other model of unseen reality that has not yet been considered may still exist that explains the known observations and facts just as well or better than the one under consideration. However, deductive reasoning can assume the hypothesis to be true and identify observations that would potentially prove the hypothesis to be false. If a large amount of evidence fails to falsify the hypothesis, confidence grows that the given model closely resembles reality.

This epistemological approach of the scientific method is derived rather than foundational because induction, deduction, and their interactive use rest on metaphysical assumptions. Inductive thought assumes that experience and observation are reliable and consistent sources of information. As we have seen, the consistency of nature, and therefore the consistency and repeatability of man's observations of it, is firmly grounded in the metaphysical reality of the Creator-creature distinction. Similarly, deductive thought assumes that man's mind is *capable* of thinking generally and rationally. This assumption, as we have seen, is firmly grounded in the metaphysical reality of the man-nature distinction, and in particular, the unique design of man. Not only are induction and deduction necessary for the scientific method, but it is the interaction between the two that gives the approach potency. That is, the scientific method assumes that man is capable of rational thought that generalizes his empirical observations in such a way that corresponds with the structural reality of nature. Indeed, the apparent accuracy of this assumption has been the marvel of many secular scientists, especially since the explosion of detailed scientific knowledge of the twentieth century.[42] It certainly is marvelous, but it is no surprise given the revealed metaphysical reality of creation. As we have seen, the Creator-creation distinction establishes that God made both man and nature and therefore the correspondence between them, and the man-nature distinction reveals that God created man uniquely with the capability of generalizing and applying knowledge of nature. As nicely summarized by Poythress, "the *a priori* capability of man's created nature really corresponds to the *a posteriori* of what is 'out there,' because man is in the image of the One who ordained what is 'out there'".[43]

As useful as the scientific method is as a derived epistemological method, it is also constrained by the limitations of man. One significant limitation certainly is the error-prone nature of man after the fall as discussed previously. There are, however, even more fundamental limitations of induction and deduction inherent in the created order. Most notable for natural sciences is man's limitations within the space-time domain. Even in the original state, each individual person's observations were limited to a relatively small space[44] and constrained by time.[45] By utilizing the scientific method and various instruments, man can extend scientific investigation beyond the directly observable in the directions of smaller and larger spaces and shorter time periods.[46] This is not possible,

---

[42] Perhaps the most well-known example of this is Albert Einstein's comment that "the eternal mystery of the world is its comprehensibility." For additional context and useful analysis of this comment, as well as similar ones from other scientists, see the chapter entitled "Why Does Mathematics Work?" in James Nickel, *Mathematics: Is God Silent?* (Ross House Books, 2001).

[43] Vern Poythress, "A Biblical View of Mathematics," in Gary North. *Foundations of Christian Scholarship: Essays in the Van Til Perspective* (Ross House, 1976), 185.

[44] Genesis 2:8.

[45] While God's actions during the creation week were instantaneous, His command to man to fill and subdue the earth (Genesis 1:28) would naturally take time to accomplish.

[46] For a nice (albeit dated) visualization of these limitations, see Julio Garrido, *Creation Research Society Quarterly*, vol. 6 (1970), num. 4: 186.

however, with longer time periods (longer than about a lifespan) because it is impossible to design repeatable experiments that could potentially falsify hypotheses about what happens (or has happened) on these time scales. Most notable to social sciences, on the other hand, is the material – immaterial boundary. As a consequence of the man-nature distinction, the study of human behavior must necessarily interact with the immaterial human spirit. While the material human body is comprised of physical components that operate in a manner consistent with the natural world around it, each living body is strongly influenced by an immaterial human soul that is completely capable of making choices and being held responsible for those choices. This means that under the exact same circumstances, two different people (or even the same person at different times) are entirely capable of completely different responses or choices. This renders the scientific method severely limited in studying the human spirit.

SCIENCE AND ETHICS

At a foundational level, ethics is informed by teleological truth. Science, then, *ought* to be employed in a manner that reflects the glory of God, which, as we have seen above, is the ultimate purpose of all things. Since God is the Creator of all, made all for this ultimate purpose, and intimately knows all that He made, it follows that God's commands for His creation (in particular, His commands for man as a unique, image-of-God-bearing, responsible creature) reveal the supreme way in which His purpose is to be accomplished. As such, man ought to heed God's commands, and his use of science is no exception.

Unfortunately, the full force of the initial foundational command of God for man is not currently in effect. Man was originally tasked to "be fruitful and multiply; fill the earth and subdue it; have dominion over the fish of the sea, over the birds of the air, and over every living thing that moves on the earth."[47] However, the catastrophic results of the fall rendered man incapable of subduing the earth and having dominion over it.[48] While the command to fill the earth is reinforced to Noah and his family after the Great Flood,[49] the command to subdue and have dominion over the earth is conspicuously absent.[50] That said, man's subduing and ruling of the earth will still be fully accomplished in ages to come under the headship of the perfect Man, Jesus Christ.[51] The exact role and therefore ethic of science in the original state and future ages is mostly speculative at this point, but as noted above, it seems very likely that generalized and applied knowledge of creation would have been (and will be) instrumental in fulfilling the dominion mandate.

Science as we know it today, on the other hand, is subject to God's foundational imperatives for man in the current age, and its role is therefore more clearly seen. To the unbeliever, the only command is to believe God's promise of eternal life through the Person and work of Jesus Christ and to thereby become a believer.[52] To the believer, many commands are given, but love of God and love of others are foundational.[53] Science, then, ought to be used in a manner that facilitates obedience to these commands. As we have seen that systematic study and generalization of nature is, in effect, listening to nature's declaration of the glory of God, science can be useful to both the unbeliever and the believer. While a systematic study of science is certainly not necessary for an unbeliever to become a believer, it may be an incredibly useful tool to a believer for witnessing to an unbeliever who is so deep in unbelief as to

---

[47] Genesis 1:28.
[48] For a full exposition of this observation see Christopher Cone, *Redacted Dominionism: A Biblical Approach to Grounding Environmental Responsibility.*
[49] Genesis 9:1.
[50] Genesis 9:2-7.
[51] Hebrews 1:8, 1:13, 2:5-9.
[52] John 20:31; Acts 16:31.
[53] Matthew 22:36-40.

deny the existence of God; the ever-increasing scientific knowledge of the intricate creation continues to declare the clearly seen attributes of God. To the believer, studying and practicing science can and ought to increase knowledge of and declaration of God's glory motivated by love of God and respect for Him as Creator. Science can also be used to love others. Indeed, as mentioned above, the use of science as a tool for witnessing is one example. More generally, though, the application of knowledge aids man in his struggle to toil against the curse on nature; it can ease burdens and temporarily prolong and increase quality of physical life. Working toward these purposes is an expression of love for others because in accomplishing them, evil can be temporarily restrained, God's grace is temporarily extended, and opportunity for the reach of the good news of Scripture is extended prior to the final judgement and commencement of the eternal state.

IMPLICATIONS FOR PSYCHOLOGY

Psychology Must Properly Interpret Observations in Terms of Its Epistemological Limitations and Metaphysical Foundations

While psychology includes major overlap with natural science,[54] it is classified as a social science because people are the primary subjects of investigation. As such, while space-time limitations certainly apply to psychology,[55] it is the material – immaterial boundary that is the primary limitation of which it must be most mindful.

---

[54] For example, the interactions of the human mind with its physical body (brain, clinical health, general development, disability, etc.) are all based on knowledge of the chemistry and biology involved.

[55] Indeed, disregard for these limitations can lead to major erroneous conclusions, such as even the very existence of the entire sub-discipline of evolutionary psychology founded upon falsely-called "knowledge" that has been declared outside of these limitations rather than scientifically discovered within them.

By way of example, it is helpful to consider one frequently used approach to handling the differences in human behavior under the same conditions: statistical sampling. Assuming a large enough random sample of people under similar conditions, observation of each individual's response to some stimulus allows for drawing statistical conclusions about human response to such a stimulus. These conclusions may start something like "on average, people…" or "the vast majority of people…" or "the typical person…". This can be valuable information for a variety of uses (especially when compared to a similar group of people who experience a different stimulus or no stimulus at all), but proper interpretation of these results depends on proper understanding of the method's epistemological limitations. It must be recognized that the underlying cause of the statistical spread in responses is altogether different from that of the statistical spread observed when observing purely natural phenomena. It is not, for example, fundamentally random differences in initial conditions or random errors in measurements (though these may be present). The first-order difference is the difference in the responsible choices of the individual human spirits (in the response itself and/or in the multitude of decisions made prior that has spiritually shaped the person).

Therefore, it can be seen that these results are not predictive of individuals, not normal or ideal, and not prescriptive. Even though typical behavior may have been observed, each individual is a responsible spirit, and the typical response cannot be used to predict how a given individual will respond. Average population-level behavior may be able to be predicted, but, for example, the counselor must take care not to apply these results as predictive of any one counselee. Furthermore, given the fallen nature of humanity, these results may be typical of the fallen population, but they are not necessarily typical of the *ideal* population (or *normal* population, as defined by the original and eternal ages). It must be understood that each human is marred by sin and brokenness. Therefore, these results cannot directly lead to prescription for what an individual, or even a population, *ought* to do. Rather, only when the results are viewed through the lens of proper metaphysical reality as revealed by the Creator can they be a useful aid in determining what ought to be done in a particular situation.

Secular Psychology Must Be Deconstructed

Since the epistemological approach of science is founded upon metaphysical truth, design of scientific experiments and interpretation of scientific observation is invariably influenced by the worldview of the scientist. Because of this and the fallen state of man resulting in his naturally rebellious disposition toward his Creator, science can be mishandled, especially by the secular scientific community. Scientific conclusions, therefore, cannot be indiscriminately taken as truth but must rather be critically examined from the Biblical worldview.

On the other hand, we have seen that the widely-used scientific method is firmly grounded in the Biblical worldview. As such, whether the scientist acknowledges proper metaphysical realties or not, the method is capable of generalizing and applying knowledge within the limits of man. That is to say, accurate scientific knowledge can be obtained by the secular scientist because he has presupposed Biblical truth in grounding his method even if he does not openly acknowledge it as Biblical truth.[56] For this reason, scientific conclusions deserve to be

---

[56] As vividly illustrated by Van Til (albeit from the Reformed theological perspective), "A little child may slap his father in the face, but it can do so only because the father holds it on his knee. So modern science, modern philosophy, and modern theology may discover much truth. Nevertheless, if the universe were not created and redeemed by Christ no man could give himself an intelligible account of anything. It follows that in order to perform their task aright the scientist and the philosopher as well as the theologian need Christ." Cornelius Van Til, *The Case for Calvinism* (Presbyterian and Reformed, 1979), 147-148.

critically examined and not necessarily discarded because of the worldview of the scientist. This is especially true of natural sciences where they stay within the space-time limitations of man.

In the case of psychology, though, the metaphysical context of the immaterial human soul (which lies beyond the reach of the scientific method) is a critical foundation to the discipline. Unfortunately, much of the current "knowledge" within psychology has been discovered (or fabricated) and interpreted by the secular community from an inaccurate worldview. The result is that much of secular psychology is misguided. Rushdoony summarizes the point of conflict well:

> It is a myth to believe that man can formulate a psychology which leaves God out of consideration, which does not begin with the fact of creation and the ethical revolt of man in the fall, and yet be in any wise an objective account of man's mind. The statement that man's consciousness has arisen out of the void by means of an evolutionary chance variation of nothing into something is not a matter of observation nor of record but of faith. It is the faith of would-be autonomous man, who insists in terms of the premise of the tempter, that he is independent of God.[57]

There will certainly be *some* observations from secular psychology that are made within the framework and limitations of the scientific method and can be useful when properly interpreted through a proper Biblical lens (for example, statistical analyses of behavior as described in the previous section). In these cases, scientific facts must be separated from unbiblical interpretations and reinterpreted appropriately. More generally, however, the prevalent psychology of today is so enmeshed in secular thought that

---

[57] Rousas John Rushdoony, "Psychology," in Gary North. *Foundations of Christian Scholarship: Essays in the Van Til Perspective.*

it must be deconstructed and a proper psychology reconstructed in its place from a Biblical worldview.[58]

The Scientific Discipline of Psychology is Firmly Grounded in Scripture

When understood properly, psychology is a discipline that ought to be explored and applied because it can be an invaluable aid in fulfilling the command to love others. It pursues the understanding of the human mind for the purpose of helping people in this current age. Hence, psychology is grounded in Biblical ethics.

It has also been demonstrated above that, when understood properly, psychology is epistemologically and metaphysically grounded in Biblical truth. The epistemological approach of the scientific method is derived from and therefore founded firmly upon key metaphysical truths revealed in Scripture (in particular, the Creator-creation distinction, the man-nature distinction, and the currently fallen state of creation). Scripture also reveals metaphysical truth that informs what questions are posed and how observations are interpreted, especially in realms outside of the limitations of man such as the immaterial nature of the human spirit.

Therefore, while secular thought has greatly influenced the discipline of psychology, it does not have an authoritative claim to it. That the secular mind would usurp the foundation without acknowledging the Creator[59] is not surprising. Indeed, the inundation of secular thought in psychology is merely part of the larger trend of the secular hijacking of science itself. Even though the birth of robust scientific thought and

---

[58] See chapter "Deconstructing Psychology."
[59] Romans 1:18-25.

process[60] corroborates the fact that its viability is *only* due to the basic Biblical understanding of reality,[61] it did not take long for "enlightened" man to use science as a veil for autonomous unbelief. However, secular thought ought *not* to have a stranglehold on psychology, for within the discipline it is *only* the Biblically-minded psychologist who legitimately stands on the sure foundation provided by the Creator.

---

[60] Of particular interest is the birth*place* of robust scientific thought, which is commonly acknowledged to be in the Christian west. In regards to the discipline of chemistry, for example, "it was only because of the new scientific outlook of the western world that chemistry did not again sink into the morass of sterile commentary and superstition that had characterized the later period of the other cultures." Henry M. Leicester, *The Historical Background of Chemistry* (John Wiley & Sons, 1956), 92.

[61] As summarized by Jaki, "European originality, which most palpably evidenced itself in science, had its origin in the Gospel, the preaching of which planted deep in European minds, long before Bacon and Descartes, the conviction that the universe was the rational product of the Creator…. The new organon of science was…in the conviction long before [Bacon] of the fact that since the world was rational it could be comprehended by the human mind, but as the product of the Creator it could not be derived from the mind of man, a creature." Stanley L Jaki, *The Origin of Science and the Science of Its Origins* (Regnery/Gateway, 1978).

5
The Sufficiency of Scripture:

Josiah Boyd., D.Min

When discussing the doctrine of Scripture, its sufficiency is typically not the first characteristic considered. Instead, its *inspiration* is rightly celebrated, its *infallibility* and *inerrancy* are appropriately defended, its *perspicuity* readily lauded, and its *authority* carefully articulated.[1] And all for good reason! Scripture *is* inspired,[2] breathed out by God himself and, originating *in* God and operating as an extension *of* God – a God who cannot lie[3] – it necessarily is without error,[4] unable to err,[5] and boasts the

---

[1] One may also consider the perspicuity of Scripture

[2] Ex 4:12–16; 17:15; Acts 4:25; 1 Cor 2:13; 2 Cor 13:2–3; 1 Thess 2:13; 2 Tim 3:16; 2 Pet 1:20–21; "The theological use of the term *inspiration* is a reference to that controlling influence which God exerted over the human authors by whom the Old and New Testament were written. It has to do with the reception of the divine message and the accuracy with which it is transcribed." Lewis Sperry Chafer, *Systematic Theology*, vol. 1 (Dallas Seminary Press, 1947), 61.

[3] Num 23:19; John 17:17; Tit 1:2; Heb 6:18

[4] Pss 12:6; 18:30; 119:89, 160; John 10:34–35; 14:26; 15:26; 16:12–15; 17:17; Jas 1:16–18

[5] Pss 12:6; 19:7; 119:89 Prov 30:5; Matt 22:41–44. "Infallibility means that something *cannot* err, while inerrancy means that it *does not* err. Infallibility describes ability or potential. It describes something that cannot happen. Inerrancy describes actuality." R. C. Sproul, "Based on God's Word Alone," in *One Foundation: Essays on the Sufficiency of Scripture* (Valencia, CA: Grace to You, 2019), 7.

authority of its Source,[6] he who is a capable communicator and, thus, understandable.[7]

God's word is authoritative *because* it is without error and it is without error *because* it is inspired by God. These pronouncements address questions of the immeasurable gravitas, unflappable trustworthiness, and divine nature of the biblical text. It's little wonder the psalmist declares to God, "I shall delight in your commandments, which I love...O how I love your law!"[8]

But what of its *scope* of influence? Does the Bible's authority extend indefinitely? Is Scripture *all* we need? And, if it is, *for what* is it all we need? Theoretically, God could have provided his people with a perfect and binding word that was, at the very same time, incomplete, in need of supplement or, at least, not opposed to supplementation. What follows is a brief explanation and defense of the *sufficiency* of Scripture, a doctrine rooted in its authority, infallibility, inerrancy, and inspiration, and one that is crucial for the people of God to not only understand *theologically* and accept *conceptually* but to apply *consistently*. Indeed, the Bible *is* enough; it *is* sufficient.

---

[6] John 10:35; Acts 24:14; Tit 2:15; 1 Pet 4:11; "If the Bible is God's Word, and God can never lie, then we have a perfect standard to embrace and obey. It is our authority. We do not have the option to reject words that are given to us from the God who never lies. We are required to submit." Heath Lambert, "Counsel the Sufficient Word," in *Sufficiency: Historic Essays on the Sufficiency of Scripture* (Jacksonville, FL: Association of Certified Biblical Counselors, 2016), 122.

[7] Scripture is described as illuminating (Ps 119:105; 2 Pet 1:19), profitable (2 Tim 3:16–17), explaining salvation (2 Tim 3:15), addressed to common people (Deut 6:4; Mark 12:37; Eph 1:1; 1 Cor 1:2), teachable to children (Deut 6:6–7; 2 Tim 3:14–15), and useful as a plumb line of truth (Acts 17:11). See Larry D. Pettegrew, "The Perspicuity of Scripture," *TMSJ* 15:2 (2004): 209–225.

[8] Ps 119:47, 97a; All Scripture quotations are taken from the *New American Standard Bible: 1995 Update* (La Babra, CA, 1995).

SCRIPTURE'S SUFFICIENCY TO WHAT END?

Before going further, space must be given to define clearly what *is*, and what is *not*, meant by the sufficiency of Scripture as some may reject or struggle with the doctrine due to a misunderstanding of its meaning and misapplication of its claims. To rightly grasp *sufficiency* one must first understand its intimate relationship with *intended purpose*. The claim that something is "enough" only has meaning relative to that for which it was provided. A teacher's salary may be adequate to meet the economic needs of a family in urban North America (that for which it was purposed) but, at the same time, be hugely *in*adequate to deal with the national debt of Italy. Similarly, a hammer is all one needs to drive nails into lumber but *not* all one needs to make a sandwich. Both the salary and the hammer are sufficient to accomplish the purposes for which they were designed and not necessarily outside of that arena. You see, a claim of sufficiency is always linked to an intended purpose. When these two concepts are divorced from one another, the result can be confusion, disappointment, or wrongful dismissal of the claim itself.[9] So, when it is claimed that the Scriptures are *sufficient*, a necessary follow-up question should be, *Sufficient for what?* or *Sufficient to what end?* or *For what purpose were they given?* In God's wisdom and providence, he has not left us guessing as to how to answer the above questions and, while space does not permit an exhaustive examination of Scriptures' self-attestation to its nature and purposes, a few key passages are briefly considered here.

---

[9] For example, if a student understands claims of scriptural sufficiency erroneously, their inability to find insights within its pages regarding modern chemistry or economics may lead them to reject the doctrine outright.

SCRIPTURE'S SUFFICIENCY CELEBRATED BY DAVID

There is perhaps no grander description of the nature, power, and purpose of the word of God then that which is provided by David in Psalm 19. After proclaiming and praising the graciousness of God in revealing his glorious self, matchless power, and inexhaustible knowledge to humanity through his creation (vv. 1–6), the king turns the attention of his pen to God's written revelation.[10]

> The law of the Lord is perfect, restoring the soul.
> The testimony of the Lord is sure, making wise the simple.
> The precepts of the Lord are right, rejoicing the heart;
> The commandment of the Lord is pure, enlightening the eyes.
> The fear of the Lord is clean, enduring forever;
> The judgments of the Lord are true; they are righteous altogether
> (vv. 7–9).

David makes use of six different titles for the Scriptures he's describing, all of which end with a statement of *to* whom they belong and *from* whom they originate "of the Lord."

God teaches his flawless doctrine throughout "the whole run and rule of sacred Writ."[11] His word is his reliable testimony, bearing perfect witness to his character and will. The Scriptures communicate God's right expectations *of* and principles *for* humanity's productivity. They are his flawless and illuminating commandments. When the Almighty speaks it is

---

[10] "The nineteenth psalm is one of meditative praise. The psalmist, looking abroad over the whole world, finds two main subjects for his eulogy—first, the glorious fabric of the material creation (vers. 1–6); and, secondly, the Divine Law which God has given to man (vers. 7–11)." H. D. M. Spence-Jones, ed., *Psalms*, vol. 1, The Pulpit Commentary (New York, NY: Funk & Wagnalis Co., 1909), 128.

[11] C. H. Spurgeon, *The Treasury of David*, vol. 1 (McLean, VA: MacDonald Publishing Co., 1975), 272.

awe-inspiring and worship-inducing and what he says faultlessly determines right and wrong.

Like examining a priceless gem from different angles, the psalmist expresses his praise for the incomparable nature of God's beautiful and multi-faceted word. It is without blemish, without equal, and without deficiency. In it God perfectly, purely, reliably, and efficaciously reveals his will, standards, demands, character, and expectations to his people. It *is* sufficient. But David doesn't stop there. Interwoven into his description of the *nature* of God's word are statements of the *functions* of God's word. Not only does he honor what the Scriptures *are* – i.e., their sufficiency – but he also eulogizes what they're *for* – i.e., their intended purpose.

According to the psalmist, God's word restores the soul and makes wise the simple. It revives that which is decaying under affliction and enlightens the otherwise ignorant. The Scriptures bring rejoicing to the heart and enlightenment to the eyes. For God's people they are not a burden but a thrill, giving wisdom and insight to the dumb and dim. What God has revealed endures forever and is wholly righteous. Its teachings, purity, and precepts are of perpetual and never-expiring obligation and, at the same time, could not be more true from beginning to end.

God's word is perfectly sufficient. But, for what? It is sufficient – lacking *nothing* necessary – for providing spiritual healing, wisdom, joy, illumination, guidance, and morality. For the purpose for which it was given, Scripture is enough.

It is of little wonder that, after this brief reflection on the nature and power of God's word, David is moved to declare his affection for it, claiming it to be "more desirable than gold, yes, than much fine gold; sweeter also than honey and the drippings of the honeycomb" (v. 10).

SCRIPTURE'S SUFFICIENCY DECLARED BY PAUL

Moving from the Old to the New Testament we come to the apostle Paul's second letter to his protégé, Timothy. Similar to David's beautiful description of the nature and function of Scripture, here we find Paul's writing on similar themes albeit more laconic.

Chapter 3 begins with a warning to Timothy to prepare for difficult days ahead, times characterized by people turning from God to godlessness, from worship of the Creator to idolatry of creation (vv. 1–9). In preparation for the coming storm of personal and ecclesial hardship and persecution, Timothy is instructed to batten down the hatches by committing himself to "the things you have learned and become convinced of ... the sacred writings which are able to give you the wisdom that leads to salvation through faith which is in Christ Jesus" (vv. 14–15). In a time marked by deception (v. 13), the young man must cling desperately to the anchor of wisdom-granting, salvation-bringing truth found in God's word.

With this need and charge as the backdrop, Paul then moves to describe for Timothy the character and capacity of these "sacred writings," i.e., Scripture, all of which "is inspired by God" (v. 16). While David poetically used six different words to describe the nature of God's word, Paul uses just one: *inspired.*

> Though the word is usually translated 'inspired,' which means 'breathe in,' technically *theopneustos* refers to a breathing out, which might more accurately be translated 'expired.' Paul is saying that Scripture is 'expired' or 'breathed out' by God. This is not a mere quibble. It is obvious that for inspiration to take place there must first be expiration. A breathing out

must precede a breathing in. The point is that the work of divine inspiration is accomplished by a divine expiration.[12]

The apostle claims that Scripture is breathed out by God and, as such, carries with it his infallible, inerrant, and authoritative character. But what of its function? What is the intended purpose of these inspired sacred writings? Paul claims they are "profitable for teaching, for reproof, for correction, for training in righteousness; so that the man of God may be adequate, equipped for every good work" (vv. 16–17).

The self-declared purpose statement of the "breathed-out-ness" of Scripture is the ample outfitting of believers—through means of teaching, reproving, correcting, and training in righteousness—to accomplish every good work they're called to accomplish. We know from elsewhere in Scripture that God has prepared good works for his people to do,[13] and here we're shown the means by which we are armed for success in those endeavors. It is via the inspired word of God that Christians are adequately prepared for their God-given tasks.

Peter echoes Paul's sentiments when he writes that, "[God's] divine power has granted to us *everything* pertaining to life and godliness."[14] The Bible, exhaled by God himself, is all that is needed for the purpose for which it was given, i.e., to prep God's people for the work God has for us to do. Simply stated, it is *sufficient* to make God's people *sufficient.*

SCRIPTURE'S SUFFICIENCY DEMONSTRATED BY CHRIST

One more passage will suffice for the purposes of this introductory chapter. While we have seen Scriptures' sufficiency

---

[12] R. C. Sproul, "Based on God's Word Alone," 4.
[13] Eph 2:10; 2 Tim 2:21; Tit 2:14; 3:8; Heb 13:21; 1 Pet 3:13
[14] 2 Pet 1:3, emphasis added

celebrated by David and declared by Paul, we now find it demonstrated by the Lord Jesus Christ.

Just prior to the start of his earthly ministry, Jesus was baptized by John in the Jordan "to fulfill all righteousness" (Matt 3:15) and, coming up from the water, in an incredible trinitarian moment, the Father spoke, the Spirit descended, and the Son was confirmed and endowed with power (vv. 16–17). However, instead of a celebration or coronation for this long-awaited King, Jesus is immediately "led up by the Spirit into the wilderness to be tempted by the devil" (4:1). While having the undivided attention of the adversary is a daunting enough thought for all who read this text, Matthew *ups the ante* in verse 2 when he discloses that "Jesus fasted forty days and forty nights" before the trial proper actually began.[15] From a human standpoint, Jesus was in a vulnerable state and it's in his seemingly diminished condition that "the tempter came" (v. 3) and began to entice the Lord to act independent of the Father's will for him. First, he tempted Jesus with his personal desire for food: "If you are the Son of God, command that these stones become bread" (v. 3). Second, Satan tempted Jesus to reveal himself to national Israel as God's Son, taking him to the top of the temple in Jerusalem and challenging him: "If you are the Son of God, throw yourself down; for it is written, 'He will command his angels concerning you'; and 'On their hands they will bear you up, so that you will not strike your foot against a stone'" (v. 6). Third and finally, the devil takes Jesus to a mountaintop view of all the kingdoms of the world. From those great heights he tempts the Lord with a universal throne: "All these things I will give you, if you fall down and worship me" (v. 9).

Three temptations were laid before an emaciated and alone Jesus. He was offered bread, something all people need. He was offered

---

[15] "As true man, He felt the intensity of physical and emotional need, experientially learning the limitations and basic drives of the human experience. Through this, He became an intercessor who feels and understands our struggles." Ed Glasscock, *Matthew: Moody Gospel Commentary* (Chicago, IL: Moody Press, 1997), 83.

recognition for who he really was, something that would inevitably occur. He was offered the kingdoms of the world, something the Messiah will eventually possess. Yet, none of these, at that particular time, was the will of the Father for the Son and, thus, they were rightly resisted. But now we notice *how* they were resisted and *how* the enemy was thwarted: with Scripture and Scripture alone. Jesus, in response to each individual temptation, reacted similarly: "It is written ... On the other hand, it is written ... Go, Satan! For it is written ..." (vv. 4, 7, 10). Each time, Jesus finds shelter in God's word. "The Lord's response to Satan's attack in the Judean Wilderness consisted exclusively of one thing—God's written revelation."[16] Jesus submits himself to the Father and the Father's revealed will for his Messiah in his word, leaning on the truth that nothing physical can truly sustain man, but only "every word that proceeds out of the mouth of God'" (v. 4). For Christ, in the throes of temptation, Scripture was enough.

SCRIPTURE'S SUFFICIENCY
AND EPISTEMOLOGICAL FOUNDATIONS

Representing the entire canon and the whole choir of biblical authors singing in harmony, David, Paul, and the Lord Jesus celebrated, declared, and modelled the divine, perfect, and truthful nature of the Bible and its subsequent sufficiency for the purposes for which it was given. What is now necessary is to move from Scripture's testimony regarding itself to application for the Christian life today. Having been reminded of the nature and purpose of God's word, we're faced with the perennial question: *How now shall we live?*

---

[16] John Adams Tucker, "Do We Really Hold Scripture to be Sufficient?," in *Dispensationalism Tomorrow and Beyond: A Theological Collection in Honor of Charles C. Ryrie,* ed. Christopher Cone (Fort Worth, TX: Tyndale Seminary Press, 2008), 192.

As has been pointed out elsewhere, "There are four major areas of philosophical inquiry that make up the basic components of worldview: epistemology, metaphysics, ethics, and socio-political philosophy."[17] Epistemology, the study of knowledge and how one knows what they know, is the primary lens through which metaphysics, ethics, and socio-political issues must be viewed, and, in that order. If an inquirer is unsure as to their *source* of knowledge, its authority, and its understandability, an exploration into the truth claims of the latter three areas and the development of a consistent worldview will be futile and yield uncertainty and insecurity. It is through the lens of a trusted epistemology that, in turn, metaphysics, ethics, and socio-political issues are rightly understood, developed, and defended.

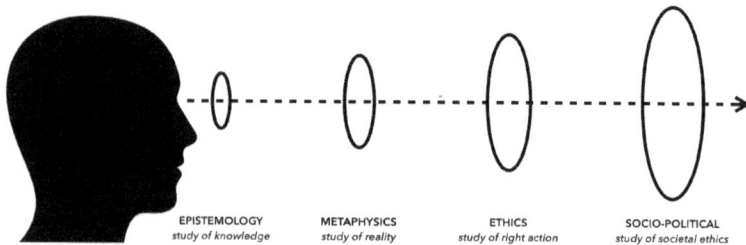

EPISTEMOLOGY   METAPHYSICS   ETHICS   SOCIO-POLITICAL
study of knowledge   study of reality   study of right action   study of societal ethics

Take the issue of capital punishment as an example. Should a nation punish individuals determined guilty of particular egregious crimes by taking their life? This is a socio-political issue, the answer to which will be rooted in a nations' answer to the question *Is it ever right to take a human*

---

[17] Christopher Cone, *Priority in Biblical Hermeneutics and Theological Method* (Exegetica Publishing, 2018), 1. Cone continues in explanation: "Epistemology (the study of knowledge) addresses the question of how can [we] know what is true and what is not. Metaphysics (the study of reality) addresses the question of what exists. Ethics (the study of what should be done) addresses the question of what we should do in light of what reality is. Socio-political philosophy (the study of ethics on a societal scale) addresses the question of how communities and society should behave."

life?, i.e., an issue of ethics. All of sudden we find ourselves back in the area of metaphysics asking questions like *What* is *human life? What* is *one worth?* and *What* is *justice?* To answer *those* questions one must appeal to a source of knowledge, i.e., an epistemology. *How do I* know *what a human life is worth? Where can I find that information and trust that information is as true as it is authoritative?* In this admittedly simplistic illustration we see that *how* one knows shapes ones' view of reality which, in turn, undergirds ones' morality and, finally, dictates how one understands the best way for people to live together in community. Thus, the starting point, i.e., the source of knowledge and the consistency to which that source is submitted (ones' epistemology), is of inestimable importance.

To put it another way: All people—whether consciously or unconsciously, intentionally or unintentionally—have a *final authority*, i.e., an epistemological foundation, to which they appeal to determine and apply truth. For children, their parents may occupy the place of final authority. For students, a favorite teacher may hold that role. For many today, "science," "scientism," or the scientific method casts the decisive vote on what *is* and what is *not* factual. For others, personal preference, emotion, and pleasure are the ultimate arbiter of truth. Whatever sits on the throne of final authority swings the gavel and declares the veracity of a truth claim regardless of its offence or disagreement with competing but lesser authorities.[18] It holds the epistemological trump card.

For the Christian, Scripture must sit on this throne consistently and unrivalled. The word of God must function as the sole foundation of *any* worldview being built; the lens through which *all* other truth claims are viewed, evaluated, and judged. Why? Because of its unique nature and

---

[18] For example, if a young man's final authority is his own desires, what his parents say, what the Bible claims, and what his friends advise will all become subservient to his ruling hedonism. It's not that they won't be heard or considered, but it's that their voices are subjected to the Louder Voice of the flesh.

its self-attested function and because of its sufficiency for the purpose for which it was given.

This is not to say that all truth not explicitly claimed in the pages of Scripture is invalid. Rather, the sufficiency of Scripture demands that all other truth claimed is filtered through, seen through, and weighed against the explicit truth revealed in its God-given pages with primacy given to that which David called "perfect…sure…right…pure…clean… true," that which Paul declared "inspired," and that which our Lord himself leaned upon in the face of alternative truth claims.

As no other source of truth has the perfect nature of Scripture, they are all insufficient as an epistemological foundation for worldview. Church history, tradition, creeds, and confessions are not breathed out by God. The scientific method, properly used, is a mere investigative tool for the exploration of a reality it has no authority to define. Human psychology, philosophy, and ideologies are all subject to the noetic effects of sin and, thus, when untethered from the infallible revelation of God are at best mistaken and at worst misleading. Personal desires, emotion, longings, and intuition are potentially deceptive and confusing as they, unlike the Bible, are marred by sin.

Again, it's not to say the above are all-together uninformative, but, without their being viewed through the lens of the inerrant word, that which was given for the express purpose of our adequacy for life and godliness, they are wholly insufficient for the task. To mold ones' view of reality, ones' moral ethic, and ones' socio-political ideology according to any errant epistemology is obviously ruinous. Scripture, and Scripture alone, is capable of filling the role of final authority and epistemological foundation.

IT'S IN THE BAG: AN ILLUSTRATION OF SUFFICIENCY

Perhaps a picture will help solidify the discussed concept in our minds. A set of golf clubs represents singularity-of-purpose and variety-of-function. A complete set includes upwards of fourteen clubs, all designed for the propulsion of a little white ball (i.e., singularity-of-purpose) but each in unique ways (i.e., variety-of-function). Some provide low and long trajectories, others high and short. Some are engineered and designed for use in sand traps, others for tee boxes, others for rough terrain, and still others for the fairway. There are clubs that will be used once or twice in a given round of golf while others will be used with much more regularity.

When a golfer steps onto any given course with a complete set of golf clubs, they are carrying with them all that they need to play the game—and play it *well*. Granted, their final score will depend on how effective they are at selecting and using the equipment they have at their disposal, but they are *in need* of nothing else. To add a hockey stick, leaf-blower, or tire iron to their golf bag would benefit them none—no matter how much they *believe* it will—and may even distract from using the proper tools at the proper times.

To bring this seemingly-abstract illustration to a hopefully useful point: What the complete set of golf clubs provides the golfer is *sufficient* for the purposes of the game they are about to play, for the *telos* for which they were designed. While proficiency with their use is another matter, a complete set of clubs provides all that is needed and all that is allowed for success in golf.

The Bible is like the Christians' golf bag – a collection of books representing singularity-of-purpose and variety-of-function. The canon was given "that the man of God may be adequate, equipped for every good work"[19] (i.e., singularity-of-purpose) and be progressively conformed to the image of Jesus Christ by the power of the Holy Spirit.[20] However, the individual books and pericopes therein present unique thrusts (i.e., variety-of-function) that all contribute to that common *telos*. Some sections will be used more than others but, when used properly and at the appropriate moments and for the purposes for which they were designed, they are ideal for the task. The skill and proficiency with which a Christian uses Scripture will vary and can be improved with prayerful practice and dependent care, but the potential effectiveness of each section of the Bible is perfect for that which it was given. To add to, take away from, or mishandle its contents is to do ourselves – and the "game" we are playing, i.e., the command to "walk in a manner worthy of the calling with which [we] have been called"[21] – a massive disservice.

SCRIPTURE'S SUFFICIENCY AND CHRISTIAN CONSISTENCY

The call for a practical doctrine of the sufficiency of Scripture is a call for Christian consistency. If the Bible *is* what it says it *is* then it follows that we must treat it as it demands to be treated: As the unrivalled epistemological foundation atop which all subsequent study *must* be built and the power by which all subsequent study *must* be fueled. As has been rightly said elsewhere, "worldview precedes observational

---

[19] Rom 12:1–2; 2 Tim 3:17

[20] Rom 8:29; 1 Cor 15:49; I understand that one could argue against the singularity of purpose for Scripture, perhaps suggesting divine self-disclosure (e.g., Pss 46:10; 119:10), the salvation of the lost (e.g., John 17:3; 20:30–31), or the mobilization of God's people (e.g., Matt 2819–20) as possible scriptural foci. Ultimately, this should be considered a tangential issue to the one being addressed here. The question is, for *whatever* the purpose it was given, is the word of God sufficient in-and-of-itself to accomplish that purpose?

[21] Eph 4:1

interpretation."[22] Thus, any successful pursuit of knowledge begins with and proceeds from a carefully established and prayerfully guarded biblical worldview.

The family of disciplines related to psychology and counselling are no exception. Probing the inner workings of people – their desires and dreams, fears and foibles, habits and hang-ups, pains and potential – *without* input from the Creator is as foolish as it is futile. Illustratively, consider this short list of questions:

- Are people fundamentally and/or basically good?
- Is suffering ever useful or deserved?
- Is morality objective?
- If immorality/evil exists, is it primarily external to the person or internal?
- What is humanity's greatest need(s)?
- What is humanity's greatest goal(s)?
- Is independence or interdependence the goal of personal maturation?
- Do people have the power to change themselves?

It should be immediately apparent that how one answers questions like these will greatly affect how one explores the human psyche and seeks to aid others in their pursuit of answers, healing, and direction. The Bible contains the divinely breathed-out answers to questions like those above[23] and, as has been already mentioned in this chapter, was given for our

---

[22] Christopher Cone, *Prolegomena on Biblical Hermeneutics and Method*, 2nd ed. (Hurst, TX: Tyndale Seminary Press, 2012), 22.
[23] For example: Rom 3:23; 2 Cor 1:3–4; 4:17–18; 1 Pet 1:16; Matt 15:15–20; 2 Cor 5:20; 1 Cor 10:31; Eph 4:16–32; Phil 4:13.

maturation in Christlikeness. Therefore, "the Scriptures are sufficient to cure souls."[24] God's word is enough.

The word of God is the final authority to which we are to appeal in all matters of life and godliness. To supplement infallible Scripture with another ideology, practice, or preference is like adding a chainsaw to your golf bag – while its novelty, perceived power, and potential usefulness may be attractive – it will at best not aid in playing the game set before us and, at worse, distract from, supplant, and replace the tools we have that were meant for such an activity.

---

[24] David Powlison, "The Sufficiency of Scripture to Diagnose and Cure Souls," *The Journal of Biblical Counseling*, Spring 2005: 2–14.

6

General Distinctives of This Approach:
Psychology and Counseling as Disciplines Born from the Biblical Worldview

Christopher Cone, Th.D, Ph.D, Ph.D

INTRODUCTION TO WORLDVIEW

In order to be sufficiently comprehensive and reliable, any thoroughgoing worldview must address four major areas of inquiry: (1) how we can know what is true or not (epistemology), (2) what is real (metaphysics), (3) what should a person do (ethics), and (4) and what should we do in community (socio-political). There is an obvious necessitated order to these questions, and that necessity should guide any discipline. We can't answer socio-political questions until we first deal with ethics, as one can't address how to behave in community if the question of how to behave hasn't first been addressed. The questions of ethics can't be answered without an adequate metaphysic that addresses what actually exists (ontology), what is good (axiology), what is the design or purpose (teleology), and what will happen in the future (eschatology).

Without having the foundational answers to these guiding questions, one could never prescribe properly. Without an accurate description of what is, one cannot instruct about what *should* be. Metaphysics answers are preface to ethical inquiry. We can't handle ethics until we answer questions of metaphysics, and we can't answer the metaphysics questions until we address the epistemological ones. Before metaphysics questions about reality, good, purpose, and the future can be answered, we have to know where to go for reliable answers. Epistemology, then, constitutes the first necessary stage of inquiry in worldview. Whom shall we trust? To whom can we go for knowledge? With what tools shall we embark on that journey? Answering these questions are the foundational role of epistemology. In particular, we must understand what is the source of authority on which the entire worldview is built, and how we can have certainty that we can properly understand that source of authority.

Components of Worldview

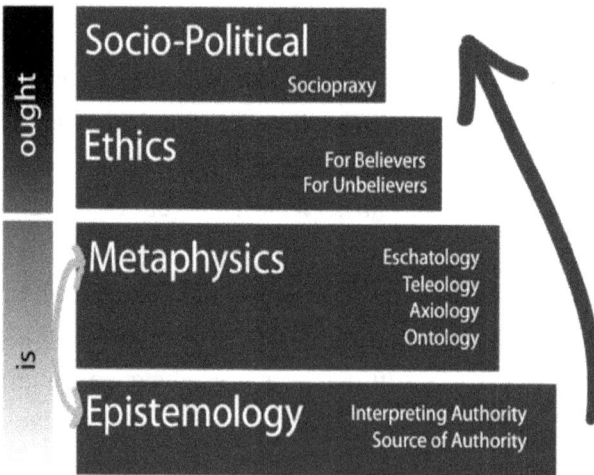

ought	Socio-Political	Sociopraxy
ought	Ethics	For Believers For Unbelievers
	Metaphysics	Eschatology Teleology Axiology Ontology
is	Epistemology	Interpreting Authority Source of Authority

Throughout the worldview investigation it is important to distinguish between that which *is* and that which *ought* to be. Descriptions of reality constitute that which is, and the prescriptions which result constitute the ought. Without answering questions pertaining to descriptions of what is, we have no basis for addressing questions of what ought to be prescribed. In any worldview, that which ought to be flows directly from what is. From descriptions come prescriptions.

It is incumbent upon any worldview, if it is to be trusted, to address each of these questions, and to do so in a way that corresponds to reality (if the resulting worldview is to reflect an accurate perspective of reality). Perhaps the greatest challenge in pursuing this metanarrative is the obvious need for a first step of faith. In pursuing foundational epistemological answers, one must decide at the outset whom or what that investigator will trust – one must take a leap of faith, basing their very first step on a pre-commitment. That leap of faith can be tested and evaluated as the worldview begins to take shape, but there is no such luxury at the beginning of the process.

Shall one trust human experience as the ultimate authority of truth, interpreting that experience through the lens of the senses? David Hume answers in the affirmative, undergirding his worldview with a naturalistic epistemology. Hume's empirical approach allows no room whatsoever for the supernatural, as his first step of faith blinds him to that possibility.

Shall one trust human reason as the ultimate authority of truth, interpreting all phenomena through the lens of guided thought? Rene Descartes answers in the affirmative, grounding his worldview with a rationalistic epistemology. Descartes' rationalism understands the phenomena independent of external voices, as reason is sufficient to comprehend the function of nature and the existence of anything beyond the natural.

Shall one trust only themselves to be the arbiter of truth, interpreting life and experience through the lens of their own existence? Friedrich Nietzsche answers in the affirmative, building his worldview on an egocentric perspective, since he doesn't believe that any other basis for meaning can be understood or trusted. Nietzsche's faith in himself, Descartes' faith in reason, and Hume's faith in experience are three common epistemological pre-commitments representative of much contemporary thought, but it is important to realize that there is another far more viable option.

THE BIBLICAL WORLDVIEW

In the Biblical worldview, the first step is faith in the Biblical God. He has revealed Himself in three ways: in general revelation through that which has been created,[1] in personal revelation with Jesus Christ the incarnate word – God revealed *in person*,[2] and in special revelation in the original autographs of the Biblical text.[3] God's revelation in nature is sufficient for all to have the knowledge of His invisible attributes, eternal power, and divine nature.[4] His revelation in Jesus Christ allows all to access the Father through the Person and work of the Son.[5] God's special revelation, the written word of God, provides all that is needed for the believer in Him to be equipped for everything He has designed His people to do.[6]

In the Biblical model, God is the Source of authority, and our worldview inquiry seeks to understand Him through His revelation in Scripture, as creation simply introduces us to Him, and His Son has revealed the Father in the written word that He commissioned.

The second task of a Biblical epistemology is to discern a hermeneutic in the Bible itself. If we have to go outside the Bible to answer this important question, then the resulting worldview is no longer rooted in the Bible. It is most helpful then that the Bible does provide a hermeneutic method that we can easily follow. In the book of Genesis are

---

[1] Genesis 1, Romans 1.
[2] John 1, Colossians 1, Hebrews 1.
[3] Proverbs 1:7, 2:6, 9:10, 2 Timothy 3:16-17, 2 Peter 1:20-21.
[4] Romans 1:20.
[5] John 6:47, 14:6, 1 Timothy 2:5.
[6] Ephesians 2:10, 2 Timothy 3:16-17.

found nearly one hundred references to God speaking, and in each of the speech acts in which the response is evident in the context, God either interprets Himself, or the other listeners interpret Him in a normative, literal grammatical-historical way. This sets a vital precedent. Genesis spans the first two-thousand years of recorded history, consequently, the hermeneutic model provided in the book is indicative of how God expects to be understood. In short, the Bible illustrates an internal hermeneutic method, and sufficiently addresses the epistemological question of how we are to interpret the source of authority.

Once the epistemological questions are resolved, the Biblicist will be able to confidently answer the metaphysics questions of ontology, axiology, teleology, and eschatology. It is in this context that we first encounter the need for psychology as a legitimate inquiry and as a discipline properly engaged within a Biblical worldview. In considering what actually exists (ontology), we are met with the Person of God,[7] who creates all that exists,[8] and thus has sovereign rights over all of His creation.[9] As the Sovereign, He defines what is good (axiology) in general,[10] and He defines what is good for His creation.[11] He determines the design and purpose for all things (teleology), and declares that all serves to express His glory.[12] As the Creator of all, He has determined the outcome and revealed much of it,[13] including His framework of covenants and promises to Abraham and his descendants,[14] His plan for

---

[7] Genesis 1:1, Psalm 14:1.
[8] Genesis 1, John 1:3, Colossians 1:16.
[9] Job 37-42, Isaiah 40:18-26, Romans 9.
[10] Genesis 1:31.
[11] E.g., Genesis 15:6, Micah 6:8.
[12] Romans 11:36, Revelation 4:11, Ephesians 1:6, 12, 14.
[13] Ecclesiastes 3:11, Isaiah 46:9-10.
[14] Genesis 12:2-3, 15:1-21, 49:10, 2 Samuel 7, Jeremiah 31.

redemption,[15] His plan for the nation of Israel,[16] for other nations,[17] and for His church,[18] His plan for the prophetic calendar and the installation of His kingdom on earth,[19] for judgment and fulfillment,[20] and for the ushering in of eternity.[21]

Within these detailed explanations of metaphysical truth is found much about the human soul and mind. God created humanity as male and female, in His image, and for His purposes.[22] He designed humanity to be spirit and/or soul,[23] and to have body, heart, soul, mind,[24] and flesh.[25] Because of the first man's sin, all who follow are stained with sin,[26] and all have a brokenness added to what God had designed – having fallen short of His glory[27] and being by nature children of wrath.[28] That brokenness includes a separation of human from Creator,[29] and physical consequences of that brokenness include dysfunction ultimately leading to physical death.[30] Those physical consequences impact not just broken humanity, but even every aspect of the physical realm is likewise stained with sin, and is profoundly dysfunctional.[31] Because of this great state of disorder, we observe all manner of maladies experienced during the times of the Biblical narrative, the foremost of which is the spiritual separation, but

---

[15] Genesis 2:15-17, 3:15, Isaiah 53, Matthew 16:21ff.
[16] Romans 9-11.
[17] Revelation 21.
[18] Matthew 16:18, 1 Thessalonians 4:13-17.
[19] Daniel 9:24-27, Matthew 24, Revelation 4-22.
[20] 1 Corinthians 3:11-15, Revelation 20:11-15.
[21] Revelation 21-22.
[22] Genesis 1:26-27.
[23] Genesis 2:7.
[24] Matthew 22:37 (Deuteronomy 6:5).
[25] 1 Corinthians 15:39.
[26] Romans 5:12-19.
[27] Romans 3:23.
[28] Ephesians 2:1-3.
[29] Genesis 2:15-17.
[30] Genesis 3:17-19.
[31] Genesis 3:17, Romans 8:22.

which also include physical ailments and illness,[32] mental dysfunction,[33] spiritual oppression and possession,[34] and the pervasive self-destructive tendencies of the flesh.[35]

The metaphysics revealed in the Biblical record are thankfully not limited to the otherwise hopelessness of humanity's sinful condition. We also discover in the narrative how God intervened in order to overcome sin and its consequences,[36] how positional righteousness and right relationship was paid for by Christ's sacrifice,[37] how those provisions are applied to the individual by faith in Jesus the Christ in the moment of justification and new birth,[38] how through the process of sanctification many of the consequences of sin are being countered daily,[39] and at the culmination in glorification the believer will see the destructive impact of sin completely resolved.[40]

THE DISCIPLINE OF PSYCHOLOGY
IN RELATION TO EPISTEMOLOGY AND METAPHYSICS

These are some of the key metaphysical descriptions found in Scripture comprising the first foundational principles of the discipline of psychology. If one ignores these revelations (as do the humanistic and naturalistic worldviews), then there is no hope for properly ascertaining a psychology that corresponds to reality. Empirical tools only provide access to a small fraction of these truths, and if those are the only tools

---

[32] Matthew 4:24.
[33] Colossians 1:21, James 1:8.
[34] Matthew 8:16.
[35] Romans 7:21-24.
[36] Romans 3:21-22, Ephesians 2:4-10.
[37] Isaiah 53:4-6, 1 Corinthians 15:1-4, 1 John 2:2.
[38] John 3:3-16, Ephesians 2:8-9.
[39] Romans 5:1-8, 6:12-23.
[40] 1 Corinthians 15:42-58, Colossians 3:3-4.

employed, then the resulting psychology will be necessarily and woefully limited if not completely errant.

It is worth noting that "science *does not* compete with Biblical epistemology, but rather ought to be an expression of Biblical epistemology. Science is only potent in particular contexts. It is abundantly descriptive of life, but doesn't decipher the origin of life. It measures functions of mind, but doesn't help us understand the derivation of mind. It does not comment intelligently on whether or not the will is free, nor does it shed light on the interaction problem – how the material and immaterial intersect, or if there is even such an intersection. The limits of science can extend only as far as the human sensory apparatus and the human reasoning apparatus intersect. As long as those who would pursue science acknowledge that limitation, the pursuit can be engaged with requisite humility, and resulting conclusions can be completely compatible with a Biblical worldview."[41] Further, the "conflict between science and the Biblical worldview arises when it is assumed that the structure and behavior of the physical and natural world is *all that exists*. That assumption demands that science is the only reliable vehicle for deriving truth and knowledge. On the other hand, where it is acknowledged that reality extends (or, at least, could possibly extend) beyond the physical and natural world, there is a humility that calls for more comprehensive tools of measure that reach beyond simply the reasoning and experiential apparatus."[42]

The core distinctions between psychology in the Biblical worldview versus the naturalistic perspectives are first evident in epistemology, with reliance on differing sources of authority. The Biblical worldview depends entirely on God as revealed in Scripture and encourages investigation through that lens. Naturalistic worldviews

---

[41] Christopher Cone, *Applied Biblical Worldview: Essays on Christian Ethics* (Fort Worth, TX: Exegetica, 2016), 12-13.
[42] Ibid., 13.

consider reason, experience, or the self as the source of authority, and pursue investigation with a very limited set of (empirical) tools. The resultant metaphysical conclusions are not shockingly disparate, because in the naturalistic model, extra-natural (Scriptural) evidence is not allowed, thus the conclusions stemming from that evidential data is discarded completely.

While psychology to this point has been considered here largely in its descriptive context (working from epistemological and metaphysical foundations), the practical value of the study is in providing prescriptions for appropriately caring for the soul and the mind. Once the epistemological questions have been addressed, one can address the metaphysical problems. Together, these inquiries comprise the descriptive, or the *is*. Once that groundwork has been laid, we move on to the *ought*, considering the prescriptions demanded by the foundational truths that have been understood. In psychology, this practical and prescriptive element related to treatment and care of the soul and mind is often referred to simply as *counseling*.

THE DISCIPLINE OF COUNSELING
IN RELATION TO ETHICS
AND SOCIO-POLITICAL INTERACTION

The Biblical worldview builds an important bridge from *is* to *ought*, from *descriptive* to *prescriptive*. Paul, for example, reveals that bridge in his letters to the Romans and to the Ephesians. Romans addresses epistemological and metaphysical questions in chapters 1-11, and in 12:1 he challenges believers in light of those foundational answers to present their bodies as a living and holy sacrifice. He further explains that this is the believer's reasonable service of worship. First outlining the description, Paul can then voice a call to action. Without the description, there is no basis for the prescription. He utilizes the same device in his letter to the Ephesians, first addressing in chapters 1-3 the epistemological and metaphysical elements related to the believer's identity, discussing at length the believer's divine calling. Then in 4:1 he calls the reader to action, "to walk in a manner worthy of the calling with which you have been called…" In both of these contexts Paul's description of reality undergirds the prescription. The description provides necessary foundations for the call to action to have significance. In both letters Paul develops a great deal of psychological material. Both deal with human identity and the reality of the human experience. Both demonstrate how God's involvement in that experience is lifegiving and empowering. Paul considers elements of the mind extensively in both letters,[43] briefly considers the soul,[44] and makes extensive reference to the human spirit.[45] That extensive psychological data helps us put into context the exhortations that comprise the ethics of the Biblical worldview.

In Ephesians 4-6, as one example, Paul offers many ethical prescriptions, but especially noteworthy with respect to counseling are the exhortations that (a) speaking the truth in love we are to grow up in all aspects of Him,[46] (b) we no longer walk in the futility of the mind,[47] (c) that we lay aside the old self, be renewed in the spirit of our mind, and put on the new self,[48] (d) that we speak only that which is edifying,[49] (e) that we be forgiving,[50] (f) that we are not be deceived by empty words,[51] (g) that we try to learn what is pleasing to the Lord,[52] (h) that we be filled

---

[43] Romans 1:28, 7:23, 25, 8:5-7, 27, 11:34, 12:2, 16, 14:5, 15:5, Ephesians 2:3, 4:17, 4:23.
[44] Romans 2:9.
[45] Romans 1:9, 8:9-10, 16, 11:8, 12:11, Ephesians 1:17, 4:23, 6:18.
[46] Ephesians 4:15.
[47] 4:17-19.
[48] 4:22-24.
[49] 4:29.
[50] 4:31-32.
[51] 5:6.
[52] 5:10.

with the Holy Spirit,[53] (i) that we speak to one another in edifying song and thankfulness,[54] (j) that we engage properly in every relationship,[55] and (k) that we understand and take up the armor of God for sustaining in spiritual battle.[56] These prescriptions are vital applications of psychological data revealed in previous chapters (1-3), and illustrate that the ethics of Scripture rely on the positional and foundational truths that comprise Biblical epistemology.

Peter, for example in both of his letters continually reminds believers of who they are, what God has done for them, and what the future holds. He does this always as a context-setting for a call to action. 1 Peter 1:1-12 considers the living hope of the believer in Christ, and the very next verse challenges the reader to prepare the mind for action and be unwaveringly fixed upon Christ. To undergird the prescription of 1:22, that believers fervently love one another, he reminds his readers of their identity (metaphysics)[57] and the trustworthiness of God's word (epistemology).[58]

Biblical counseling is one way we "stimulate one another to love and good deeds,"[59] applying the epistemological and metaphysical foundations of Scripture in ethics (individually) and socio-political interaction (in community). In the Biblical worldview there are two essential recipients of ethical prescriptions. First is the unbeliever. Biblical ethics for them is fairly straightforward: their primary responsibility is to believe in Him. Biblical ethics for the believer is much more detailed, as there are perhaps more than one-thousand directives in the New Testament for believers to follow. The purpose of Biblical counseling is

---

[53] 5:15-18.
[54] 5:19-20.
[55] 5:21-6:9.
[56] 6:10-18.
[57] 1 Peter 1:23.
[58] 1:24-25.
[59] Hebrews 10:24.

to encourage one another to be more like Christ in our thinking, our speaking, and our actions, thus counseling can play a helpful and needed role in the sanctification process for believers. For unbelievers, Biblical counseling can help them with their primary directive: to believe in Jesus. While counseling can be of great help to unbelievers as an expression of common grace, the overarching desired outcome is that they become new creatures who have the mind of Christ,[60] and are indwelt by the Holy Spirit.[61]

While not all aspects of psychology are not merely descriptive, and not all aspects of counseling are merely prescriptive, generally, the descriptions of the Biblical model for psychology lead directly to the Biblical prescriptions for counseling. If the psychological data and foundations are rooted in a different worldview – Hume's, Descartes', or Nietzsche's, for example, then the counseling prescriptions will necessarily look very different.

CONCLUSION

The general distinctiveness of the model we are advocating is that it be rooted in and engaged through Biblical authority as the fundamental epistemological truth, with the Biblical descriptions providing the essential metaphysical concepts through which we understand human psychology and undergirding the prescriptions for the purpose and approach to counseling. Observation and scientific pursuit are very important, and as long as their limitations are acknowledged, they can be invaluable tools in properly applying the metaphysical concepts presented in Scripture. If on the other hand, we fail to put those tools in their proper place as limited devices for considering the metaphysical principles' impact on human experience, then we begin to mishandle and distort the

---

[60] 1 Corinthians 2:16.
[61] Ephesians 1:13-14.

two first stages of worldview, and we are no longer operating anywhere close to the Biblical worldview.

It is necessary that we do psychology according to the Biblical worldview *without* integrating any other competing worldview concepts with the Biblical foundations. If we embark on this journey faithfully guarding those boundaries, then we can be assured of coming much closer to understanding that which corresponds to reality as the Creator designed and sees it than we otherwise would if we add our own limited perspectives whether they be extra-biblical theological presuppositions or secular pre-commitments to leave Him out of the equation altogether.

Just as Paul cautions believers not to be taken captive through philosophies not according to Christ,[62] we must examine every aspect of our worldview to assure alignment with His word. Any time we step outside the boundaries of His worldview, we are no longer engaging in the philosophy according to Christ but are instead being captivated by competing worldviews – by empty deceptions.

---

[62] Colossians 2:8.

7

Specific Distinctives of This Approach:
Consistent Application of the Literal Grammatical Historical Hermeneutic

Luther Ray Smith Jr., Psy.D

INTRODUCTION

Among believers in the body of Christ who practice counseling there are many methodologies and approaches to counsel from. All of them, in one way or another, assert that their particular method they subscribe to in the service of advising counselees is "biblical." One may adhere to a particular teaching because of what the Scripture communicates on that subject. Others may observe an instruction because a person of high standing within the counseling community teaches this perspective. There may be others who may lean on both sources and choose which one is best to use according to the situation the counselee expresses. At the same time many of these approaches that are stated as being "biblical" appear to be in contention within one another, stating that each one lacks certain biblical qualities which should be included in their perspective of counseling. One practice may state that the counselee's conformity to the Law (i.e., "The Ten Commandments") is the goal of counseling, while others state the purpose of counseling is just "to get people well" so they can live fulfilled lives. Others may claim the objective of counseling is for those to know their negative thought patterns so they can change their thoughts and in effect change their behavior, while others may believe the goal of counseling is to explore one's traumatic memories so that can be emotionally and cognitively restored. What are the various approaches that are found within counseling and how does a biblical counselor know what approach is biblical? How can a biblical counselor know that they are being guided by a truly biblical ethic? This chapter will explore the foundational presuppositions of the biblical worldview and the significance of why these must be within the explanation of a "biblical" approach. The various models found within counseling will be investigated, paying special attention to the foundational source of each model, the subject focus of the counseling model, the aspect or time of each counseling model, and the "biblical focus" of these various models.

THE FOUNDATIONS OF A BIBLICAL EXPLANATION

There are various explanations of the word "biblical." One such person describes the word "biblical" as an approach one must take with their life, with their central reference being the Bible when this author wrote the following:

> Being biblical, then, means approaching the Bible as the story that shapes our whole life. As God's authoritative story, the Bible invites us to inhabit its storied world because it's the truest understanding of the world that's possible, and then to comport ourselves accordingly. Being biblical means being shaped to the core of our being. That includes our lifestyles, habits, decisions,

thoughts, beliefs, even our most intimate hopes and dreams and the means by which we seek to make them a reality.[1]

The previous explanation stated that the Bible is a story, which shapes the very core of a person who believes its instruction. What are the fundamentals that are needed to recognize whether a teaching is biblical? This writer submits four core presuppositions, explained below, to give an explanation of the term "biblical:"

1. **God exists and that He has revealed His attributes in creation**: Nature, and all that is made reveals that there is a Creator. By observing creation, we understand that the genesis of all things comes from God, and that this Creator is not a product of the things that this Creator has made. Nature reveals that this God created the world with order and design. Furthermore, it is also seen that there is organization in regard to nature and how things work (e.g., creatures bearing the same kinds of creatures). Lastly, we observe that there is a function and purpose to all that this Creator has made (e.g., the sunlight causes plants to grow). It appears that nature's purpose is to display the power, creative work and order of God. Although Creation is great to tell us about the powerful and awesome work of this Creator, it is insufficient in that creation does not tell us personally who this God is and this God's desire for mankind.

2. **God exists and He has revealed Himself personally to mankind by the means of speech, and language**: God, by His own will, has chosen to reveal Himself personally to mankind. He has revealed Himself throughout history, sometimes in very

---

[1] Michael Wagenman. *What Does It Mean to Be Biblical?* 2008. Retrieved from https://www.thebanner.org.

dramatic and unique ways (c.f., Exo. 19:18-25). Furthermore, He has also revealed Himself, and His plan through His Holy Spirit by means of the Scriptures (2 Pet. 1:20-21). This account given by God to mankind would include the Old Testament and New Testament.

3. **God exists and has created mankind with the ability, through the use of speech and language, to understand His Self-Revelation**: God has chosen to communicate to mankind by the use of speech and language.[2] Mankind has also been given the ability by God to understand the usage of words and grammar. Mankind has been given the capability to reason, to think and ponder the structure and form of the words that have been written, and that rules for grammar and language would also be constantly applied. Mankind has the capability to understand and comprehend the meanings of words so a person may understand what God was intending to communicate about Himself and how one should live.

---

[2] It is interesting to note this is a detail that is repeated in the Scriptures. When God commands Adam not to eat of the tree of the knowledge of Good and Evil He does so by way of speaking (Genesis. 2:14). The usage of the term "God said" in the book of Genesis is used 87 times. The phrase "The LORD said" is used 19 times. Essentially God speaks over 100 times in the book of Genesis alone. Furthermore, God communicates by way of speech to Noah, Abraham, Isaac, and Jacob. Even when the Lord appeared in miraculous ways God still communicated who He is and His will by way of speech and language (c.f., Exodus Chaps. 3-5;20:1a). God, thorough Moses, communicated the origin of creation and the birth of the nations and Israel by way of words and language. When the Lord raises the prophets up to address the nation of Israel through speaking to them. When Jesus, God in human flesh, says "I say to you" He does so collectively in the Gospels 128 times emphasizing God communication to man with language. When the disciples of Jesus are witnesses of Jesus they communicate the teachings of Jesus using speech and language. Paul, when writing to Timothy states that the written word (i.e., Scripture) is "breathed out" by God Himself underscoring that God has chosen to communicate with language to mankind (2 Timothy. 3:16).

4. **The consistent understanding of these words to understand God's Self-Revelation**: The words that God communicated to man were intended to be consistent throughout the biblical text. The words, meanings and definitions of these words, were to be understood and comprehended in their plain and normal sense within the context that these words were written in.[3]

These four points above are the criteria that make up a true explanation of what "biblical" means. In light of our inquiry for a counseling model to be genuinely biblical it must acknowledge that there is a God that exists, and that His attributes are seen and observed in creation (c.f., Rom. 1:18). The model must understand that God has communicated personally with mankind, and He has done so by the use of language and speech (i.e., by His word). The model must also understand the basic rules of grammar and the consistent meanings of the words in the bible and their relation to the immediate and overall context of Scripture. In other words for a counseling model to be biblical it must *not* only focus on the doctrinal, and theological stances that influence the counselor and perhaps the counselees worldview, but the *method* one uses, and the *consistency* of the method a person uses, to arrive at the conclusions of their doctrinal or theological positions. Every model used in counseling is reinforced by a philosophical system concerning the substance and function of mankind, and the process one uses to arrive and reinforce the philosophy of the counselor is extremely important.

---

[3] This is also an example that is observed in Scripture. When God spoke to mankind, mankind always took His word in its plain sense. This is seen with Adam and Eve (c.f., Genesis 1:28; 2:17), Cain (Gen. 4:6-7; 11-15), Noah (Genesis chaps. 6-7:1-5; 9:1-17), Abraham (Genesis 12:1-3; 15:1-8), Jacob (Genesis 28:13-15), Moses (Exodus. 3:1-15), Joshua, (Joshua 1:1-9), David (1 Samuel 7:8-16), Isaiah (Isaiah 6:8-13), Ezekiel (Ezekiel 4:1-8), Daniel (Daniel Chaps. 10-12), just to name a few. The apostles in their writing of the epistles also took God's word in its plain sense when God spoke (c.f., Acts 13:2) .

MODEL #1: THE "GOD IS NOT" MODEL[4]

The "God is not" model is found within counseling. This model embraces the philosophy of Secular Humanism, a progressive philosophy of life that, without theism or other supernatural beliefs, affirms our ability and responsibility to lead ethical lives of personal fulfillment that aspire to the greater good.[5] The philosophy in this model is underscored when Paul wrote,

> For the wrath of God is revealed from heaven against all ungodliness and unrighteousness of men who suppress the truth in unrighteousness, because that which is known about God is evident within them; for God made it evident to them. For since the creation of the world His invisible attributes, His eternal power and divine nature, have been clearly seen, being understood through what has been made, so that they are without excuse. For even though they knew God, they did not honor Him as God or give thanks, but they became futile in their speculations, and their foolish heart was darkened. Professing to be wise, they became fools, and exchanged the glory of the incorruptible God for an image in the form of corruptible man and of birds and four-footed animals and crawling creatures (Rom. 1:18-22 NASB).

The philosophy in this model actively suppresses the characteristics of God's attributes by concluding mankind is just an evolved animal (in the case of Darwin), or is only a biological machine that responds to inner

---

[4] The reason I am including the "God is not" model in counseling is because it is one of the perspectives that is used within counseling. So even though it is a viewpoint that is not contentious to the truth claims of Scripture, this author for the sake of comparison felt it necessary to include it in this analysis.

[5] American Humanist Association. *Definition of Humanism*. (American Humanist Association, 2022). Retrieved from https://americanhumanist.org.

drives or external stimuli (in the case of Freud, Skinner, & Pavlov). Furthermore, the source of authority that one answers to when they adopt this particular view is the research methods that observe natural phenomena (i.e., Scientism), and secular humanistic theorists and theories found within the discipline, because they are the experts that specialize in human behavior. In addition, when it comes to natural observations about human behavior they may make astute observations, because they are observing creation that is made with order and design. However, because of their suppression of the reality of God they come to incorrect conclusions about the substance and function of mankind. Lastly because they reject the reality that God exists they naturally reject how He has communicated His will with mankind and how one is to observe the world around them.

MODEL #2: THE "ASSIMILATION" MODEL

This model seeks to take the best observations and techniques from theorist and researchers in the discipline of psychology and incorporate them to the theology of the Scriptures. In other words, they attempt to "assimilate" the observations found in psychology with theology. One such author noted this when he wrote the following:
By way of analogy, consider the temperature system in an automobile. On one end of the continuum is hot air and to the other end is cool air. Often a person selects a temperature in the middle, mixing the hot and the cool air for the desired effect. The climate is more desirable and adaptable by combining both sources of air than it could be if only one source of air were available...in this analogy we are considering two sources of information: psychology and the Christian faith. To what extent should he let the "air" from both systems mix to achieve an optimal balance? Or should we trust only one source of information and not the other?

Reciprocal interaction involves the assumption that caring for people's souls is best done by bringing together truth from both sources.[6]

Some who adopt this particular model may be convinced that the discipline of psychology informs their theological positions as one such author commented, "I believe that psychology plays a significant role in analyzing theology. Psychology offers explanations and definitions for behaviors in connection to Christian ethics. Psychology verbalizes our theological feelings and behavior. Psychology helps to understand our theological narratives and the reasons behind them."[7]

Other Christians who operate with this particular model state that problems that humanity faces are complex and the blending of the doctrines of Scripture, combined with Secular techniques may not completely restore a person, but it provides the greatest opportunity for their needs to be addressed. As this case with this author below:

The use of some secular therapy interventions is not inherently wrong; the overreliance and/or independent use of these techniques is. Research and personal testimonies reveal that secular interventions are successful in the abatement of symptoms. However, the independent use of these secular techniques falls short because they simply produce a "symptom free" individual. The end result does not provide dependence on the Lord, salvation, or sanctification. The result is nothing more than freedom from current symptoms, yet there is continued bondage to sin. The underlying cause of pathology (separation from God) has not been addressed. Therefore, we cannot eliminate the Gospel from therapy. We also cannot discard all secular techniques.[8]

---

[6] Mark McMinn & Clark Campbell. *Integrative Psychotherapy: Toward a Comprehensive Christian Approach.* (Intervarsity Press, 2007). 23.

[7] Jonah Waseberg. *The Dialogue Between Psychology and Theology.* (The American Association of Christian Counselor, 2022). Retrieved from https://aacc.net.

[8] Sarah Rainer. *Psychology vs. Scripture: 5 Reasons to Glean From Both.* (2014). Retrieved from https://churchleaders.com.

Additionally, some believers who operate with this mindset are convinced that the Scriptures should govern over the methods and techniques found in psychology, as one such counselor wrote, "We can profit from secular psychology if we carefully screen our concepts to determine their compatibility with Christian presuppositions."[9]

The sources of authority found in this counseling position either takes the observations found within the discipline of psychology and attempts to explain or interpret theological doctrines from this position, or it seeks to take the best from both worlds, recognizing the benefit from research and theorists and utilizes them to assist the counselee. Those who employ this model make proper observations concerning the physical aspects of mankind and acknowledges the immaterial aspects of mankind. The focus of a counselor who subscribes to this perspective is two-fold: Counselors use the research and theories to assist counselees with relation to the *material* aspect of man. However, in terms of spiritual matters counselors will use the Scriptures to address the *immaterial* aspect of mankind. [10] Furthermore, this model does accept the word of God as special revelation. It does not seek to suppress the truth of God, who He is, and what He has created as in the case of a "God is not" model for counseling. Rather this particular model seeks to promote the benefit of extra-theological sources that do not oppose the truth in Scripture in caring for the biological, social, and cognitive needs of mankind.

---

[9] Larry Crabb. *Effective Biblical Counseling*. (Zondervan, 1977). 48.

[10] It would appear some who subscribe to this view only view the spiritual as salvific, as the case with Dr. Reiner when she noted the following: "I acknowledge that all humans are inherently separated from God. This separation causes disorder, sin, and disease of every kind. However, we serve a loving and just God that provides a way out of our depraved state through Jesus Christ. He longs for us to seek Him and His promise of eternity." (Sarah Rainer. *Psychology vs. Scripture: 5 Reasons to Glean From Both*. (2014). Retrieved from https://churchleaders.com).

MODEL #3: THE THEOLOGICAL MODEL

This particular model of counseling (sometimes referred to as "Biblical" counseling) believes that the Bible (i.e., sound theology) should govern the perspective and the praxis of counseling. Proponents of this model observe the word of God as authoritative and sufficient. The explanation of sufficiency is espoused by these writers when they wrote the following:

Perhaps there is no better summary of the Bible's teaching about our complete sufficiency in Christ than the one given by the apostle Peter when he wrote that by His divine power, God "has granted to us everything pertaining to life and godliness (2 Pet. 1:3). "Life" has to do with everything related to living effectively and biblically in our daily activities and relationships with our environment with other people. "Godliness" has to do with our relationships with God—with living a God-centered, God-conscious life marked by godly character and conduct.[11]

Proponents of this model also strongly discourage the use of the findings and the theories in psychology, which these authors underscored as they wrote, "Psychology and theology have never been comfortable bedfellows. Their basic philosophical presuppositions are almost diametrically opposed to each other. Psychology rests upon a secular (humanistic or naturalistic) view of man's problems and solution to those problems, and theology rests upon a biblical view of man and his problems. The basic anthropology and theology is at opposite ends of the intellectual spectrum."[12]

As mentioned above those who subscribe to this perspective believe the central component of counseling is theological. This view is expressed by an author when he wrote, "Counseling is a theological

---

[11] Wayne Mack. *Totally Sufficient.* (Harvest House Publishers, 1997). 51.
[12] Ibid.

discipline. There."[13] In a further discourse to extend on this idea he continued this thought:

> Understanding that counseling requires some vision of life is crucial to understanding the theological nature of counseling. The reason that is such a vision of reality is always theological. God defines what it is to be and a human being, and He describes that in his Word. God knows what is wrong with us and diagnoses the problem in the Bible. God prescribes a solution to our problems—faith in Christ— and reveals him to us in the Scriptures. God authorizes a process of transformation and shows us what it looks like in the pages in of the Old and New Testaments.[14]

A website dedicated to biblical counseling espoused this position when they detailed the following: "We believe that biblical counseling is fundamentally a practical theological discipline because every aspect of life is related to God. God intends that we care for one another in ways that relate human struggles to His person, purposes, promises, and will. Wise counseling arises from a theological way of looking at life—a mindset, a worldview—that informs how we understand people, problems, and solutions. The best biblical counselors are wise, balanced, caring, experienced practical theologians."[15]

Another quality to note is that even though they reject some of the theories in light of counseling and psychology those who advocate this particular perspective of counseling do not reject biological causes to problems. One such supporter of this model wrote, "I do not wish to

---

[13] Heath Lambert. *A Theology of Biblical Counseling: The Doctrinal Foundations of Counseling Ministry.* (Zondervan, 2016). 1.

[14] Ibid.

[15] Baylight Counseling. *Confessional Statement.* Retrieved from https://www.baylightcounseling.com.

disregard science, but rather I welcome it as a useful adjunct for the purpose of illustrating, filling in generalizations with specifics, and challenging wrong interpretations of Scripture."[16] Another such author commented, "...biblical and Christian counselors agree that psychologist make true observations that are often helpful. This really is an area of agreement. Few have doubted that Christian counselors embrace this view. Many have doubted that biblical counselors agree with it...In spite of all of the accusations in this regard I am aware of no biblical counselor who outright rejects the findings of psychology..."[17]

The sources of authority found within this particular movement are the sacred Scriptures and theology (specifically systematic theology).[18] Like the "Assimilation" model of counseling they recognize Scripture and have a high regard for it. Consequently, they see mankind as being material and immaterial in nature, with the overarching problem of mankind being (active) sin. Their primary aspect is the eternally focused as they seek to evangelize the world with counseling.[19] They embrace theological

---

[16] Jay Adams. *Competent to Counsel: Introduction to Nouthetic Counseling* (Zondervan, 1970). xxi.

[17] This has been a statement that is made by those who subscribe to a theological model of counseling. However, when this particular statement is made there is very little explanation about what scientific or psychological information, they find helpful to use with this modality. In fact it could be said that while they say they support some of the findings of psychology they spend much time warning or discouraging people away from the discipline (Sironi 2010). It would be beneficial for counselors who advocate this model to describe what information they find helpful in the discipline to adopt in their counseling practice.

[18] Theological positions that are promoted in this view are usually observed in the light of a *theological tradition* outlined in Confessions and Creeds (i.e., the Westminster Confession), rather than the just the Scriptures. This will be explained later in this inquiry.

[19] This is one of the prominent affirmations found on a biblical counseling website which underscores the following point: We believe that Christianity is missionary-minded by its very nature. Biblical counseling should be a powerful evangelistic and apologetic force in our world. We want to bring the good news of Jesus and His Word to the world that only God can redeem. We seek to speak in relevant ways to

positions and seek to use those doctrinal and theological truths to serve those counselees and bring them healing.

A MISSING ELEMENT IN ALL THREE MODELS

All of these models attempt to address the ills that plague mankind. The "God is not" model views mankind as nothing more as a living machine or a bipedal animal, and that the purpose of counseling is essentially to give people the tools to live fulfilled lives and achieve a sense of self-worth and purpose. The "Assimilation" model views mankind as a physical and spiritual being and uses methods and techniques depending on what aspect of man is being addressed. For the physical (biological, social, and cognitive), there are techniques that researchers and theorists have developed in an attempt to address these material issues. The goal of counseling in this model is similar to the "God is not" model in that the counselor seeks to equip the counselee with the tools to live purposeful lives here. For the spiritual issues this model seeks to use the Scriptures to address this particular issue of man (i.e., the redemption of the counselee to God the Father through Christ). The "Theological" model also sees man as dualistic but seeks to resolve the ills of man completely through the wisdom of systematic theology. The goal of this particular counseling is ultimately to conform the counselee to live a life of godly conduct and worship. However, each of these models examined have a missing element that makes them incomplete from being observed as a biblical model, as outlined in the author's explanation, and that is the mention of the *hermeneutical method* that each model uses.

The "God is not" model rejects the idea of the existence of God, therefore it fails to satisfy the other three requirements that are found in the biblical explanation, as mentioned above the philosophy found in this

---

Christians and non-Christians, to draw them to the Savior and the distinctive wisdom that comes only from His Word (Biblical Counseling Coalition n.d.).

model is hostile to the reality that God has revealed His qualities in creation.

The "Assimilation" model of counseling does acknowledge that God does exist, and that His order is seen in creation. They recognize that God has revealed Himself through His word, and that His word is meant to be understood. However, this model, by and large, does not focus on a consistent hermeneutical method either, but observations concerning theorists and theological doctrines. As a result, this creates three problems: 1) This model affirms that the observations found in the discipline should interpret the Scriptures. This is backwards as psychology is a discipline of study, and it is our philosophy that informs how one observes the discipline. 2) This model assumes, whether knowingly or unknowingly, that the biblical worldview *lacks* in addressing an aspect of mankind. The "Assimilation" model presupposes that believers need to *add* the spiritual component of man, rather than recognizing it is the "God is not" philosophy that has *removed* the spiritual aspect of mankind. Consequently, this creates a bifurcation in the "Assimilation" counseling philosophy stating that counselors can use "secular" methods to counsel counselees for material purposes, and the word of God for spiritual purposes. Counselors who use the "Assimilation" model neglect to see the philosophy that governs the motive over the methods used to address material and immaterial problems are underscored in Scripture, and that the techniques that work for counselees are being *borrowed* from those who have a "God is not" philosophy. 3) the "Assimilation" model does acknowledge *that* psychology is a discipline that must come under the authority of Scripture, but it does not describe a consistent biblical hermeneutical method (other than systematic theology) by which the discipline can be observed.

The "Theological" model of counseling affirms all of the details mentioned concerning the biblical explanation described. However, the deficiency found in this model is somewhat similar to the one seen in the

"Assimilation" model. They promote that counseling is mainly theological, and that doing good theology is important to the practice of counseling. However, this begs two questions: *How* does one do good theology and how does one *know* their theology is good? Good theology is not established by past or present theologians, creeds, catechisms, confessions, or church traditions.[20] But it is the consistent hermeneutical method of reading the Scripture that should establish a counselor's theological positions, govern their worldview, and guide their rationale. All of these models are inconsistent in one degree or another to meet the standard of "biblical" because each model falls short to explain what hermeneutical method, they employ that governs their conclusions. As a result, all of these modalities do not meet the qualifications as being truly biblical.

MODEL #4: A BIBLICAL APPROACH

There is a fourth model that this writer believes meets the criteria for a truly biblical model for counseling. First the Scriptures (i.e. special revelation) combined with the consistent normal grammatical historical method of observing and explaining the Scriptures is the source of authority of how one builds their counseling perspective. This gives the counselor the viewpoint in observing creation in its proper place, which includes mankind as male and female was created by God on day six of creation (Gen. 1:24-29; Gen. 2:7, 2:21-23). As a result, the counselor, employing the consistent hermeneutic observes mankind as material (Gen. 2:7a; Ps. 139:13-16a) and immaterial (Gen. 2:7b), and because God has created both aspects of man, both qualities are seen as important in

---

[20] Now I am not suggesting that these are not helpful. What this author is attempting to express is that the comments these men made concerning Scripture, as impactful as they are, are not inspired. Additionally, these things establish knowledge concerning the Scriptures by rote information, but they do not teach a consistent hermeneutic as to how to read Scripture.

the counseling process. Those who employ this method understand that the observations of creation, specifically the ones observed concerning mankind, belong to the believer as mankind, and mankind's activities, emphasize the attributes of God (Rom. 1:18). A consistent methodology also emphasizes the problem of mankind as seen by the fall, and the implications of this as expressed in a sinful nature (Gen. 3:16b; Rom. 3:10-18), and the *passive effects* of the fall of mankind (c.f., 1 Thess. 5:14d). Furthermore, a consistent hermeneutic establishes discernment amongst the findings and techniques in the field of psychology, where findings observed in the natural order (e.g., the brain and is connection to emotional and physiological responses) may be recognized to emphasize God's created order, and are used by the counselor without prejudice. The ideas that are fanciful and are against the Scriptures (which usually are *philosophical* in nature) are discarded (c.f., Col. 2:8; 2 Cor. 10:4-5). Additionally, the counselor using this methodology understands that counseling is not only salvific, but extends to assist the counselee in all faculties mankind possess (thought, word, and deed), understanding that God's word does not only address redemption from sin, but *how* to live in the world (c.f., Prov. 1:1-7). The counselor, who subscribes to the consistent method of observing the Scriptures knows that to do good for the believer and unbeliever is something that God desires, caring for their material and immaterial needs (Gal. 6:10). This approach due to the method of reading Scripture focuses on God's revealed word exclusively, directing the counselor's decisions in how they guide their counselees in any situation.

The benefit is that this method focuses on a "God-is" reality in both creation and His revealed word (in contrast to the "God is not" model). It also uses the consistent normal grammatical hermeneutical method to examine theories and the perspective of theorists against God's word (in contrast to the "Assimilation model). This model seeks to rely on the consistent hermeneutical method of explaining and understanding the Scriptures directly in their plain sense from the biblical text, not beginning with theological positions (in contrast to the "Theological" model).

CONCLUSION

What should it mean when a counselor says that they are "biblical" in their counseling? From a brief examination of the word it includes several characteristics: 1) God exists and His attributes are seen in creation, 2) God has personally revealed Himself by use of words and language, 3) God has given mankind the ability to understand His communication, and 4) His communication is meant to be understood consistently through proper use of the rules of grammar, and the meanings of words consistently. The "God is not" model fails to meet these criteria because it denies the very existence of God. The "Assimilation" model, although close, fails to meet the criteria because it fails to outline a consistent hermeneutical method it uses to govern over the discipline of psychology. The "Theological" model much like the "Assimilation" model is close, and yet fails to meet the criteria because it starts with a theological system instead of a consistent hermeneutical method. This is what makes this biblical counseling model distinct from all other models mentioned. This model does not primarily focus on theories and theorists, systematic theologies or confessions, but the counselor who adopts this view builds and establishes their biblical worldview of counseling using a hermeneutical method consistently from the Bible, guiding the rationale of their techniques and observations in diagnosis to assist the counselee in their needs, all for God's glory. Amen.

Soli Deo Gloria!

8
The Bible, Psychology, and Education
Allan Henderson, Ed.D

.INTRODUCTION

The purpose of this chapter is to show that those who are seeking to engage in Biblical Counseling ought to experience cross-training from different academic fields to encourage them to think comprehensively about the discipline and other related disciplines. As a result, the Biblical Counselor can become a competent practitioner finding his or her ultimate authority in Scripture, while utilizing carefully examined secondary sources to inform their practice. This chapter examines the purpose and function of a discipline and academic field, the means of educating to promote the Biblical worldview, and the application of a scholarly practitioner in the field.

Education is often viewed as a means for development in three specific domains: the cognitive domain, the affective domain, and the behavioral domain. Each domain contributes to the process of equipping a person with the tools to become a productive citizen in the sense of being able to function in society according to its customs and standards, which can be called *cultural norms*. A contributing factor to this outcome is a curriculum that is put together by persons who want to influence the way a student thinks, feels, and behaves. Although there is no consensus on the definition of *curriculum*,[1] there are key components that are identifiable. Curriculum should include goals and objectives, content, learning strategies, and assessment.

Exchanging the term curriculum for academic plan, Lattuca and Stark correctly note that curriculum development can be a difficult task because of the lack of unanimity regarding its definition and that the problem can be further exacerbated by a curriculum committee that consist of people from different disciplines or academic fields.[2] In an attempt to conceptualize a harmonious approach to curriculum development or revision, they identify eight essential elements of an academic plan (curriculum) that could be used for developing an academic program, which are: purpose, content, sequence, learners, instruction, evaluation, and adjustments. These elements, if addressed in the development of a curriculum on the program level, would help with cross communication among faculty from different disciplines or academic fields, so that their collaboration would produce a well-rounded graduate.

THE PURPOSE AND FUNCTION
OF A DISCIPLINE AND ACADEMIC FIELD

In education the words *field* and *discipline* are often used interchangeably. However, some scholars differentiate between the two, viewing an academic field in an inclusive sense and a discipline as more restrictive.[3] In other words, *disciplines* can be grouped under academic *fields*. In this sense, there is an overarching philosophy that that influences the way a student acquires knowledge within a given discipline. To this point,

---

[1] Lisa R. Lattuca & Joan S. Stark. *Shaping the College Curriculum: Academic Plans in Context* (Jossey-Bass, 2009), 1.

[2] Ibid., 3.

[3] Ibid., 89.

Lattuca and Stark recognize four academic fields: humanities, science, social science, and professional studies as being typical across institutions of higher learning on the undergraduate level.

An academic field provides a framework for one to use as a means to examine the external world and the discipline within that field trains one how to pursue specific knowledge. Examining the different academic fields: humanities, science, social science, and professional field, one would see that a particular way of acquiring knowledge is characteristic of a particular field. For instance, humanities as an academic field has a construct of promoting critical thinking. In addition to critical thinking, the disciplines under humanities are geared toward training people to think deductively. Such a thought finds support in Helen Small's description of humanities. In her book, *The Value of Humanities*, she discussed the epistemological aspect of humanities as being one of interpretation and critical evaluation among other aspects.[4]

In-regards to academic disciplines, Biglan developed a typology that consist of three dimensions to help categorize disciplines, which are: hard/soft, applied/pure, and life/non-life.[5] The significance of these categories helps one to recognize the value of an academic field and discipline in conjunction with the application of knowledge. Disciplines that belong to the hard stratification are those that have more of a unified structure with epistemology. In other words, hard fields have codified standards by which those within that field adhere to as essential

[4] Helen Small, *The Value of the Humanities* (Oxford: Oxford Press, 2013), 23. https://eds-b-ebscohost-com.proxy.library.maryville.edu.
[5] Willis A. Jones, "Variation among Academic Disciplines: An update on Analytical Frameworks and Research," *Journal of the Professoriate*, 2012 Vol. 6 Issue 1, p 9-27, Academic Search Complete.

knowledge. Thus, hard disciplines have a definitive paradigm that is used to provide answers or a method of inquiry for examining a phenomenon.[6]

Those disciplines that belong to the soft domain on the other hand tend not to have a strong consensus on what constitutes appropriate research questions and methodologies to address such research questions.[7] Biglan's model, which developed from research by faculty from different disciplines from public and private colleges or universities yielded academic disciplines such as philosophy, psychology, and anthropology, for example, as soft disciplines. The typical university curricula model would recognize philosophy as belonging to the humanities field, and psychology and anthropology as belonging to the social science field.

Although the categorization of academic disciplines as being either being hard or soft was the most vital aspect to Biglan's research, the category of applied/pure is essential in ascertaining the value of an academic field. Disciplines that belong to the applied domain have more applicable knowledge to real life situations. In other words, practical application of the knowledge gleaned from such disciplines are of great importance. Disciplines that fall under the pure category are more likely to advance basic knowledge than showing the practical aspect of the subject matter.[8] Thus, it can be said that the two different schemes reveal the disparity between practice and theory.

The distinctions of hard/soft, and applied/pure is germane to the discussion of what constitutes Biblical Counseling because of the value these domains bring to education. Human constructs are not authoritative like the Bible, but they often help to deepen one's understanding of a

---

[6] Anthony Biglan, "The Characteristics of Subject Matter In Different Academic Areas," *Journal of Applied Psychology*, 1973 Vol. 57 Issue 3, p 195 – 203, https://doi.org/10.103/h0034701.

[7] Willis, "Variation among Academic Disciplines," 11.

[8] Lattuca and Stark, *Shaping the College Curriculum*, 93.

particular subject matter. Biglan's model of academic discipline classification is not infallible, but offers several ideas pertinent to the subject of Biblical counseling. With that said, theological systems and educational theories are constructed by humans and are thus limited, but those limitations do not negate their value to humanity.

Essentially, there are only two premises that exists as being foundational to any discipline. The first is the creationist perspective which views life as a creation from a Creator. The other view is secular-humanist in that it denies the existence of a Creator, thus making life a microcosmic organism that evolved over time. This bifurcation has a tremendous impact on the methodology for inquiring knowledge. To this point, science, as an academic field typically utilizes a secular-humanistic premise for acquiring knowledge.

On the other hand humanities as an academic field consists of a broad range of disciplines that may or may not include the study of God; scholars within humanities study the process whereby knowledge of phenomena is applied by the culture.[9] Jonathan Bates, suggests the value of humanities using the story of Joseph found in Genesis 41.[10] Although Bates denies the authenticity of the story of Joseph, he uses it to show the importance of being able to interpret narratives as a literary critic.[11] The ability to interpret literature helps one to understand culture. He adds, for example, the disciplines of linguistics, paleography, history, archeology, and theology are essential to communicating humanity's need for divinity.[12] It is interesting to note that he did not mention the need for God, but for divinity, which denotes some skepticism pertaining to the existence of a personal God who has revealed himself through the Bible. While Bates is on the secular-humanistic end of the spectrum, not all

---

[9] Small, *The Value of the Humanities,* 23.
[10] Jonathan Bates, *The Public Value of the Humanities* (London: Bloomsburg Academics, 2011), 1. https://eds-a-ebscohost-com.proxy.library.maryville.edu.
[11] Ibid., 1.
[12] Ibid., 1.

scholars within these fields reject the premise of creation or the premise of a personal God.

The discipline of theology does not necessitate a belief that the Bible is the word of God. There are theologians who reject the notion that the Bible is a divine book and hold that it is only a collection of stories to help us promote the good of humanity. There are also those who believe that the Bible *contains* the word of God, meaning that there are portions of the Bible that are not inspired. Others recognize the verbal and plenary inspiration of Scripture, meaning that the Bible in every aspect is a divine book. To this regard, not all conclusions in the discipline of theology are equal because theology is a human construct, varied depending on one's view of Scripture and the implementation of an interpretive system (hermeneutics) of the Bible. As such, when we consider what makes Biblical counseling Biblical, we conclude that a major facet is viewing the Bible as completely authoritative and thus interpreting it as its Author intended.

THE MEANS OF EDUCATING
TO PROMOTE THE BIBLICAL WORLDVIEW

Developing the biblical worldview is a lifetime process of reexamining, redefining, and ultimately changing a way of thinking contrary to the teachings of the Bible. Paul addressed this issue in 1 Corinthians 8:1-8. Addressing the Corinthians about food that was offered to idols, Paul began the discussion by cautioning about pride that can originate from knowledge.[13] A practical application of Paul's teachings in these two verses shows the value of a Biblical worldview in education.

If education is done correctly, it can be a humbling endeavor, if the goal is to learn. Learning a subject can be dangerous at the onset when

---

13 8:1-2.

one is learning the basics because those on a basic level do not yet know what they should know. As one continues to deepen one's knowledge base in a subject then he or she begins to learn that there is a lot more to the subject than what is known by them. In their pursuit of knowledge he or she may come to realize that there is always more to be learned. Nevertheless, the information that is being learned ought to correspond to the Biblical worldview, which Paul was demonstrating.

Verse 4 connects the thought of growing in knowledge with the topic of eating things offered to idols. Paul asserted that there is only one God, a truth underscored in Deuteronomy 6:4, which reads, "Hear, O Israel, The Lord God is our God, the Lord God is one." Understanding that there is only one God according to the Scriptures, some in the Corinthian church concluded that it is not problematic to eat food that was sacrificed to idols. This is the precise reason why Paul told them not to allow their liberty to eat food sacrificed to idols to become a stumbling block to others who think differently.[14] However, it is essential to point out that Paul viewed the issue of eating food sacrificed to idols as a nonbinding issue for Christians, and one that shouldn't cause contention. This finds support from verse 8 which reads, "But food will not commend us to God; we are neither the worse if we do not eat, not the better if we do eat."

Once again, it is vital to let the Scriptures inform one's theology, which would consequently inform one's practice. Theology is a discipline that everyone who has the ability to reason, practices without even knowing they are doing so. Everyone has questions or thoughts about human life and its purpose.[15] All human beings who are able to communicate through any modality have expressed and will continue to

---

[14] 8:9.
[15] Stanley J. Grenz and Roger E. Olson, *Who Needs Theology?* (InterVarsity, 1996). 15.

express a theology that can be judged as being vile or good by using the Bible as the evaluative tool.

There are those who are a part of a theological tradition that teaches the superimposing of a theological conjecture onto the biblical text. There exists a method of interpreting the Bible called the *theological interpretation*, which makes an attempt to show the relevance of theology to people outside of the academy. According to Nate Dawson, theological interpretation helps to integrate the role of theology with scriptural interpretation.[16] However, the concern is making theology the priority in the exegetical process. Charles Ryrie evaluates the theological interpretation as failing to maintain a consistent plain reading of the Biblical text. Moreover, Christopher Cone pinpointed a critical and longstanding problem of creating a divergence between Biblical scholarship and theology.[17] In addition to this observation, Cone rightly concludes that both are dependent on each other and if one is not exegetically sound then one is not well equipped to make theological claims.[18]

Learning to critically evaluate a text for its intended meaning is a skill set that is gained through the academic field of humanities (and hermeneutics, to be specific). While keeping Paul's sentiments about growing in knowledge,[19] we must recognize that those disciplines that are constitute humanities are only a piece of the puzzle. The field itself has limitations. For one to become more knowledgeable about other areas of life, a basic understanding of other academic fields is important. Therefore, a brief synopsis of the following academic fields is essential to

---

[16] Nate Dawson, "Making the Shift to Theological Interpretation of Scripture," *Anglican Theological Review*, Vol. 99 Issue 4 (2017) p753 – 762, 10p. Page 756. Master File Premier.

[17] Christopher Cone, *Priority in Biblical Hermeneutics and Theological Method* (Exegetica Publishing, 2018). 78.

[18] Ibid., 78.

[19] 1 Corinthians 8:2)

our discussion. Those fields include Social Science, Science, and Professional Fields.

Social Science should be an important expression of the Biblical worldview, because of the skill sets that one can gain from this academic field. Although it requires more subjective analysis than does the field of Science, it can be more objective than the Humanities, seeking to draw conclusions through analysis of data. Unfortunately, some tend to rely on anecdotes as a means to verify a claim because they have not been trained to make decisions based on empirical research. A major distinction between Social Science and Humanities is the type of data that is being analyzed. It appears that Humanities focuses more on historical research, while Social Science focuses more on empirical research. The Social Sciences teach one how to study a phenomena in its natural occurrence.

Diversity, for example, illustrates how the social sciences are beneficial to helping one express the Biblical worldview. We live in a pluralistic world with people from all walks of life, and yet we are called to pursue peace with all men.[20] A good way to pursue peace is by seeking to understand those who are different from us. Peter taught husbands to live with their wives in an understanding way.[21] Scripture gives husbands a framework to work from for living with their wives, but it does not give them the details on how to carry that out because women differ in their attitude and behavior although there are commonalities due to the Fall. Thus, men must be able to study their wives in their natural occurrence, meaning not as a controlled variable, in order to understand them. Such actions can be ascribed as qualitative research. It would be best for a husband not to live with his wife by relying on anecdotal conclusions.

On a grander scale, the implications of the social sciences can be seen in Acts as the church was growing. At one point, the early church mainly consisted of Hebraic and Hellenistic Jews. Luke recorded an

---

[20] Hebrews 12:14.
[21] 1 Peter 3:7.

incident where the Hellenistic Jews raised a complaint against the native Jews because the Hellenistic Jews' widows were being neglected with respect to the daily distribution of food.[22] Why were they overlooked? History informs us that animosity did exist between the two groups because of cultural differences. Some believe that this incident was not deliberate,[23] but there is no evidence in the text to support such a conclusion. Also, we are not told exactly how the complaint got to the apostles, but the mere fact that one group was mistreated within the church reveals the need to understand life from the perspective of other people groups so that valid concerns can be addressed. It is not enough for the Christians to assume such behavior does not exist among believers. Social Sciences has helped the church to reexamine much of her behavior that was previously overlooked due to assumptions, disbelief, and disregard.

Science as an academic field can help one think objectively and inductively by examining the specifics and then drawing a conclusion. In this sense, a hypothesis is made and then tested, and the results of the experiment could either prove or disapprove the hypothesis. In other words, Science as an academic field is more objective in its analyses of data than is Social Science, and Humanities. As such, this academic field trains one to avoid gray areas, but to search for facts. In short, it combats a philosophical teaching that truth is relative. However, this is not to say that scientists draw irrefutable conclusions. Instead, science helps us to discover laws that God designed during creation, which magnifies God's infinite wisdom and exposes the finitude of the human mind. To this point, William Yount noted that science seeks to increase our knowledge about the processes God set-forth during creation.[24]

---

22 Acts 6:1.

23 John B. Polhill, *Acts* in The New American Commentary vol. 26 (Broadman & Holman Publishers,1992) 179, Logos.

24 William R. Yount, *Created to Learn: A Christian Teacher's Introduction to Educational Psychology* (Broadman & Holman, 1996), 29.

Christians must be careful in thinking that the Bible is a science book because it is not. However, as rationale beings we can study the creation which is not limited to the physical things we can see or observe. The opening verse of Genesis simply reads, "In the beginning God created the heavens and the earth." What follows in the creation account of Genesis is a brief description of some physical things that were created, and not so much of what was necessarily implemented to make life function. Science can inform us about the functionality of certain things that are essential to life, like the atom or the anatomy of the human body. Social Science can inform us about the functionality of certain things that are essential to life, like relational interaction and understanding cultures and morays. The Humanities can inform us about the functionality of certain things that are essential to life, like ideas of truth, concepts of origin, and ethical prescriptions.

Expanding our knowledge base to include information that is presented to humanity from the different academic fields makes one a well-rounded learner. Moreover, one does not have to be an expert in every field, but should learn to respect and engage the information that scholars representing different disciplines across each academic field produce. This is vital because no one individual can be a content specialist in everything. It is beneficial to have a basic knowledge of information produced from the distinct fields of the academy, particularly when viewed through the Biblical lens.

THE APPLICATION OF A SCHOLARLY PRACTITIONER
IN THE PROFESSIONAL FIELD

A distinguishing factor between the professional field and the other academic fields is one of practicality in the sense of finding practical applications to theories.[25] As such, areas of practice under the professional field seek to bridge the gap between theory and practice. This is a distinguishing characteristic because unlike the other academic fields, the professional field trains a person to address problems that are geared towards the provision of a service, which is more client based, whereas the other academic fields train one to address questions and inquiries that are only fitting for a particular discipline.[26] In other words: science, social science, and humanities are not presumed to be concerned with deriving knowledge from each other. The professional field, on the other hand, is presumed to have an interdisciplinary value.

An examination of the work done by several scholars on the classification of academic discipline, including Biglan's, has revealed that none of the research has taken into account the characteristics of the professional field.[27] In part, the dismissal of including the field may be due to its uniqueness and an ideology that the practicality of a discipline should not be the concern of the academy because graduates would get the practical aspect of their education from working in the field.

The argument between the two philosophies of education is centered on the acceptance or rejection of pragmatism. Historically, pragmatism concerned itself with the central assumption that what constitutes truth is gained through experiential means.[28] There is a sense where one can learn truth through an experience, but one should not

---

[25] Lattuca and Stark, *Shaping the College Curriculum*, 93.

[26] Ibid., 93.

[27] Ibid., 93.

[28] Tricia Smith, "Pragmatism" in *Educational Theories*, (Salem Press, 2014), 13, https://eds-b-ebscohost-com.proxy.library.maryville.edu.

affirm truth in the absolute sense through experience. However, another emphasis of pragmatism within education today is the development of life-long learners.[29] Growth and learning consist of correcting any beliefs or assumptions that were based on previous knowledge, or the lack thereof, and corrected or expanded by new information gained through the learning process.

Biblical counseling can be viewed as a professional ministry in the sense that formal training is needed in order to help practitioners correctly utilize the Scriptures in a counseling session. Thus, this area of practice should be classified as a professional field since practitioners are offering a specialized service that requires methods of inquiry from more than one academic field. As noted by Lattuca & Stark, and other scholars, academic fields shape the way a person seeks and validates knowledge.[30] Therefore, Biblical counselors ought to be familiar with different methods of inquiry taught by the different academic fields as means to inform their practice. So much information that can inform a Biblical counselor's practice has gone forth from disciplines such as: neuroscience and human anatomy and physiology which are categorized in the field of biological science; anthropology and psychology, which are categorized within social science; and theology, which is categorized as part of humanities.

It is important to note that informing one's practice does not necessarily mean that there is an agreement with the conclusion of the research. An example of this may be the observations made by psychologist or anthropologist on a population that demonstrate certain behaviors that are response to a certain action. Such information made be appropriate when counseling someone who would fit the characteristics of that observed population. In using such information to inform their practice, Biblical counselors will be doing the work of scholarly practitioners.

---

[29] Ibid., 13
[30] Lattuca and Stark, *Shaping the College Curriculum*, 96.

The creed of one particular approach to Biblical counseling is found in 2 Peter 1:3, which has been used to support the notion that the Bible alone provides the truly Biblical way to counsel:

> ...seeing that His divine power has granted to us everything pertaining to life and godliness, through the true knowledge of Him who called us by His own glory and excellence.[31]

On the other hand, there is nothing in 2 Peter 1:3 that excludes the use of other sources of knowledge in a counseling situation. In this verse, Peter is not dealing with counseling or restricting one from gaining knowledge outside the Scriptures. Peter does deal with sanctification (being set apart from the power of sin) as being only possible through the knowledge of Jesus Christ. Hence, when Peter mentions that God bestowed upon believers His precious and magnificent promise,[32] this included the promise of the Holy Spirit to indwell all who have believed in Jesus.[33] That each believer is indwelt with the Holy Spirit is significant. Without Him a person will not have the ability to overcome the power of the flesh.[34] To this point, 2 Peter 1:3 does not restrict a person to using the Bible alone in a counseling situation. It does, however, signify the importance of grounding all counseling on the Bible since it is the word of God and is contrary to worldly wisdom.[35] Therefore, the Biblical counselor can judge through the Scriptures the information gleaned from other sources to determine whether or not the information can help inform one's practice.

---

[31] *New American Standard Bible: 1995 Update* (The Lockman Foundation, 1995), 2 Peter 1:3.
[32] 2 Peter 1:4.
[33] John 7:38-39.
[34] Galatians 5:16-17.
[35] 1 Corinthians 2:12-15.

CONCLUSION

Examining what makes Biblical counseling Biblical, extends beyond the use of the Scriptures as the counselor's final authority. Those who study the Bible and allow the Bible to construct their theology would recognize that all humanity is made in the image of God, although all are flawed. Because of this truth, a Biblical counselor should not have a problem with engaging or utilizing information from other disciplines that are grouped under different academic fields. Since each field has a unique way of contributing to the value of life by training people to acquire knowledge through various methods of inquiry, it would serve the Biblical counselor well to be knowledgeable of their research findings.

By virtue of having been created in God's image, scholars from different disciplines can contribute something beneficial to a counseling situation. However, a good Biblical counselor, while using such information to inform their practice, will know how to rightly discern by evaluating everything through the Scriptures. They will be able to decipher between Biblical and anti-biblical ideas. Hence, Biblical counseling is a professional field that should maintain the integrity of the Scriptures as the word of God and that should be comprehensive in its approach.

9

The Authority and Sufficiency of Scripture
And The Role of Extra-Biblical Resources In Transformative Teaching and Learning[1]

Christopher Cone, Th.D, Ph.D, Ph.D

INTRODUCTION

Paul affirmed to Timothy the authority, capacity, and sufficiency of the Scriptures for the adequacy of the believer.[2] In similar fashion Jesus applied the sufficiency of Scripture in responding to His testing by Satan. Yet in close proximity to both instances we observe the employment of extra-Biblical resources in complementing the situation. In Paul's case, even as he exhorts Timothy to faithfulness in the word, he acknowledges value in Timothy's attentiveness to not only what Paul taught and wrote, but to his experiences as well.[3] In Jesus' case, He acknowledges there is a

---

[1] Initially presented to the Bible Faculty Summit, BJU, Greenville, South Carolina, August 1, 2018, and subsequently published in *Interdisciplinary Journal on Biblical Authority* Volume 1, Number 1, Spring 2020: 16-45.

[2] 2 Timothy 3:16-17.

[3] 2 Timothy 3:10-11.

place for bread, though it ought not be viewed as the sole source of life.[4] Likewise, after His testing He was the beneficiary of angelic ministry.[5]

In both instances, the word of God is affirmed as authoritative and sufficient, and in both situations, other resources help to set or complete the context. Considering these and other Biblical scenarios, this paper evaluates the nature of Biblical authority and sufficiency and the role of extra-Biblical resources in transformative teaching and learning. To underscore the practical value of the authority and sufficiency issues, this study also compares principles observed in the Biblical narratives with principles employed in psychology and counseling, providing a case study for the application of extra-Biblical resources in transformative teaching and learning contexts.

THREE VIEWS OF AUTHORITY AND TRADITION

Within Christianity there are three primary perspectives on the relationship of Biblical authority and Biblical tradition. The first (B+T) views the Bible as authoritative, but also views Tradition (with a capital T) as provided by God and as equally authoritative. The Roman Catholic Church (RCC), for example, embraces this approach. The second (B+t) views the Bible as authoritative, but views tradition (little t) as a necessary hermeneutic lens through which to view the Bible. Reformed and Covenant theology take this view. The third (B+Ø) holds to the idea that the Bible is exclusively authoritative, and that while tradition is important for understanding contexts and interacting with people, it is neither a source of doctrinal authority nor a hermeneutic aid. This third approach is distinctive in its a commitment to applying *sola scriptura* in every area of faith and practice.

---

[4] Matthew 4:4, from Deuteronomy 8:3.
[5] Matthew 4:11.

Bible Plus Capital-T Tradition (B+T) [6]

While both Catholic and Protestant teachings affirm the authority of the Bible, there are two significant distinctions between the Catholic and Protestant understandings of how exclusive the Bible's authority actually is. First is found in the extent to which the analogy of faith applies. In Protestant methodology, the analogy of faith is understood as Scripture interpreting Scripture, whereas in Catholic methodology, there is a higher opinion of extra-biblical material – the explanations and declarations of the teaching authority of the church. On this, the Catechism explains that, "The whole body of the faithful…cannot err in matters of belief,[7] and because the Church is our mother, she is also our teacher in the faith.[8] "The Church…does not derive her certainty about all revealed truths from the holy Scriptures alone. Both Scripture and Tradition must be accepted and honored with equal sentiments of devotion and reverence."[9]

The second major difference is in the related ideas of *ex cathedra* and apostolic succession. In Catholic understanding, the Church is built on Peter, the unshakeable rock of the church.[10] Thus from Peter the church gains her authority, and the Popes derive their *ex cathedra* authority. In Protestant understanding, Jesus is the rock upon which the church is built, being the rock of offense, and a fulfillment of Isaiah 8:14, as acknowledged by Peter in 1 Peter 2:8. This variance in interpretation sets distinct trajectories for both groups – Catholics finding revelation to extend beyond the biblical text, and Protestants, asserting that revelation goes no further than the completed texts that Jesus affirmed and

---

[6] Portions of this section adapted from Christopher Cone, "Authority of Scripture and Hermeneutic Method as Historical and Continual Bases for Christian Unity and the Collaborative Avenues They Imply," a paper presented to the Florovsky Week Symposium, Newman University, Wichita, Kansas, July 11, 2018.

[7] Catechism, 92.

[8] Ibid., 169.

[9] Ibid., 82.

[10] Ibid., 552.

commissioned. Consequently, the divergent epistemological moorings contribute to the disparate (and at times violently so) theological conclusions.

Catholic exegetes defined both the direction and the method to be followed in the task of understanding the Scriptures,[11] which entailed investigation and explanation through the study of original languages and reliance on original texts.[12] However Pius XII acknowledged that especially during the middle ages, theologians lacked the requisite knowledge of Hebrew and Greek, and found themselves reliant on the Latin Vulgate.[13] Instead of availing themselves of "the aids which all branches of philology supply,"[14] scholars during that time had limited resources and limited knowledge. But, asserts Pius XII, like Jerome, we ought to "explain the original text which, having been written by the inspired author himself, has more authority and greater weight than any even the very best translation, whether ancient or modern; this can be done all the more easily and fruitfully, if to the knowledge of languages be joined a real skill in literary criticism of the same text."[15] Thus attention to the biblical languages and to textual criticism become central to understanding Scripture. Pius XII was emphatic regarding the necessity of and demand for such scientific study of the text:

> this prolonged labor is not only necessary for the right understanding of the divinely-given writings, but also is urgently demanded by that piety by which it behooves us to be grateful to the God of all providence, Who from the throne of His majesty

---

[11] Pope Pius XII, "Divino Afflante Spirito," Paragraph 9.
[12] Ibid., 14.
[13] Ibid.
[14] Ibid., 16.
[15] Ibid.

has sent these books as so many paternal letters to His own children.[16]

Pius XII is careful to mention that the Vulgate still has great value (as emphasized in the Council of Trent),[17] and was perhaps even preferable in some sense, since it had been "approved by its long continued use for so many centuries in the Church."[18] Because the Vulgate was "free from any error whatsoever in matters of faith and morals…it may be quoted safely and without fear of error…so its authenticity is not specified primarily as critical, but rather as juridical."[19] Still, for the making clear of doctrine, the authority of the Vulgate "almost demands either the corroboration and confirmation of this same doctrine by the original texts or the having recourse on any and every occasion to the aid of these same texts."[20]

Because Jerome included apocryphal books in his Vulgate translation, (possibly based on their inclusion in the Greek Codex Sinaiticus) those books remain an esteemed component of the Catholic Bible. These texts are typically rejected by Protestants on grounds that they are historically separated from the Hebrew OT, and based on some of the doctrinal conclusions the apocryphal books derive.[21] These disputed texts represent a point of division between Catholic and

---

[16] Ibid., 19.

[17] Ibid, 20.

[18] Ibid., 21.

[19] Ibid.

[20] Ibid., 22.

[21] E.g., 2 Maccabees considers prayer and sacrificial offerings for the dead, the merits of the martyrs, and intercession of saints; Tobit 12:9 and 14:11 seems to suggest that almsgiving purges sin; 1 Maccabees 2:52 suggests that Abraham's passing the test was reckoned to him as righteousness, not his believe in the Lord (as in Gen 15:6); 2 Maccabees 12:41-45 presents the doctrine of purgatory; and 2 Maccabees also considers sacrificial offerings for the dead, the merits of the martyrs, and intercession of saints, etc.

Protestant, as the Council of Trent in 1546 codified the Apocrypha to be inspired, cementing that aspect of disagreement.

While English translations of the OT contain around 600,000 words, and the NT contains around 175,000 words, the Apocrypha includes about 160,000. Because the Apocrypha is nearly the size of the NT, the textual basis for Catholic and Protestant disagreement is not insignificant, nor are the doctrinal distinctions unimportant. The most severe of these differences is evident in the context of how a person is justified before God.

Virtually every single one of Luther's *95 Theses* pertain to issues relating to how one is justified, and the implications for remission of sins, purgatory, papal authority, the use of indulgences, etc. Luther was largely protesting what he perceived to be a taught doctrine of salvation by works, and added to his translation of Romans 3:28 the word "alone," in order to ensure the understanding that justification comes by faith alone. On the other hand, Catholic soteriology agrees that "Believing in Jesus Christ and in the One who sent him for our salvation is necessary for obtaining that salvation,"[22] and "without faith no one has ever attained justification."[23] Still, that "We can lose this priceless gift"[24] illustrates that justification, in the Catholic soteriological system, is not by faith alone.

The Catholic hermeneutic also has at its core a commitment to the literal meaning of Scripture. Pius XII's exhortation to that end provides no lack of clarity:

> Being thoroughly prepared by the knowledge of the ancient languages and by the aids afforded by the art of criticism, let the Catholic exegete undertake the task, of all those imposed on him the greatest, that namely of discovering and expounding the

---

[22] Catechism, 161.
[23] Ibid.
[24] Ibid., 162.

genuine meaning of the Sacred Books. In the performance of this task let the interpreters bear in mind that *their foremost and greatest endeavor should be to discern and define clearly that sense of the biblical words which is called literal*. Aided by the context and by comparison with similar passages, let them therefore by means of their knowledge of languages search out with all diligence the literal meaning of the words; all these helps indeed are wont to be pressed into service in the explanation also of profane writers, so that the mind of the author may be made abundantly clear [emphasis mine].[25]

Still, just as there is attention given to the literal aspect of the text, there are other hermeneutic commitments that distinguish the Catholic hermeneutic. The Second Vatican Council prescribes three criteria for interpreting Scripture: "1. Be especially attentive to the content and unity of the whole of Scripture…2. Read the Scripture within the living Tradition of the whole Church…3. Be attentive to the analogy of faith."[26] In these three criteria is evident the value attributed to tradition as a vital lens through which to view Scripture. Further, the Protestant hermeneutic is well represented by Luther's assertion, quoted by Farrar, that "The literal sense of Scripture alone is the whole essence of faith and of Christian theology,"[27] whereas the Catholic methodology upholds a plurality of senses in Scriptural meaning: "According to an ancient tradition, one can distinguish between two senses of Scripture: the literal and the spiritual, the latter being subdivided into the allegorical, moral, and anagogical senses. The profound concordance of the four senses guarantees all its richness to the living reading of the Scripture in the church.[28]

---

25 Pope Pius XII, "Divino Afflante Spirito," 23.
26 Catechism, 112-114.
27 Frederic Farrar, *History of Interpretation* (London: McMillan and Co., 1886), 327.
28 Catechism, 115-117.

In these contexts – understandings of what constitutes Scripture, the exclusivity of biblical authority, and hermeneutic methodology, the essential source of authority is ultimately not the same for Protestantism and Catholicism. If in a biblical worldview the source of authority is God as revealed in the Bible, then the Bible is the final and unaugmented record of God's outline for worldview, including descriptive aspects of epistemological and metaphysical concepts, and prescriptive aspects of the ethics and socio political thought.

In a Catholic worldview, the source of authority is still recognized as the biblical God, but He reveals Himself in more diverse ways than simply the pages of the Bible. Consequently, there are differences between Catholicism and Protestantism in both the descriptive elements of worldview (epistemology and metaphysics) and the prescriptive elements (ethics and socio-political).

Bible Plus Little-t Tradition (B+t)

Cornelius Van Til is astute on three significant pillars of Biblical epistemology: (1), the Biblical God exists, (2) He has revealed himself authoritatively, and (3) Natural man's incapacity to receive, but his epistemology falls short in that he does not account for hermeneutics (Pillar 4) *within* his epistemology. In fact, in his Th.M thesis, "Reformed Epistemology," Van Til does not discuss Biblical interpretation. Much of his critique of other thinkers, like Kant, includes considerable discussion of their deficiencies in the interpretation of experience, but not a word about method in interpreting Scripture. It is surprising to this writer that Van Til would build such an outstanding foundational framework on special revelation and then totally ignore the centrality of hermeneutic method for understanding that revelation, because Biblical hermeneutics as an absolutely necessary component of epistemology. In his *The New Hermeneutic*, Van Til concludes, with these words, "...we would appeal to the Cahier's men, to Wiersinga and to others, *to build their hermeneutical procedures on the theology of Calvin, Kuyper, Bavinck, etc.*, (emphasis mine) and then in terms of it to challenge all men to repentance and faith in the self-identifying Christ of Scripture instead of making compromise with unbelief."[29] Notice his prescribed hermeneutical procedures are grounded in historical theology, rather than literal grammatical-historical. In short, Van Til is marvelously consistent in his epistemological method until he prescribes historical theology as the orthodox hermeneutic, rather than literal grammatical-historical (an unfortunate contradiction of his own expertly stated first principles).

Van Til's hermeneutic maneuver is not quite as overt as the RCC hermeneutic prescription that is emblematic of B+T, but it certainly requires that Scripture be viewed through the lens of tradition, and consequently illustrates a B+t methodology – the methodology employed particularly in Reformed/Covenant theology. Kevin DeYoung likewise illustrates the Covenant/Reformed starting place as (at least) little-t, tradition: "As a Christian I hope that my theology is open to correction, but as a minister I have to start somewhere. We all do. For me that means starting with Reformed theology and my confessional tradition and sticking with that unless I have really good reason not to."[30] DeYoung's methodological reliance on systematic theology becomes an integral part of his hermeneutic. "Without a systematic theology how can you begin to know what to do with the eschatology of Ezekiel or the sacramental language in John 6 or the psalmist's insistence that he is righteous and blameless?"[31] The implications of DeYoung's hermeneutic are evident in his remarkably nonliteral handling of the 144,000 in Revelation 7 as the

---

[29] Cornelius Van Til, *The New Hermeneutic* (Philipsburg, NJ: Presbyterian and Reformed, 1974), 180.
[30] Kevin DeYoung, "Your Theological System Should Tell You How to Exegete," The Gospel Coalition, February, 23, 2012, viewed at https://www.thegospelcoalition.org/blogs/kevin-deyoung/your-theological-system-should-tell-you-how-to-exegete/.
[31] Ibid.

"entire community of the redeemed."[32] DeYoung understands the quantity simply as "a way of saying all God's people under the old and new covenant,"[33] and he understands the entire context as "stylized to depict the totality of God's pure and perfectly redeemed servants from all time over all the earth."[34]

While Van Til and DeYoung do not attribute inspired authority to tradition (as does the RCC), their handling of Scripture does not reflect much practical difference. In practice, B+T and B+t are closely related.

Bible Plus Nothing (B+Ø)

The related ideas of a completed canon and the superior reliability of revelation over personal experience are important bases for *sola scriptura* in understanding and in application. Peter illustrates the principle of revelation trumping personal experience when he explains that even though he had witnessed Christ in His glory at the transfiguration,[35] the prophetic word regarding Christ – or God's revelation – confirmed the issue.[36] What Peter says on this subject is important, because even if God did presently use experiential or sensory means, it would be secondary to His word. Peter also describes in those verses how God spoke to people – the Holy Spirit moved men to speak the word of God.[37] Certainly, God did speak to people in dreams and other ways.[38] And Paul agrees that all Scripture is God-breathed.[39] Still, in 1 Corinthians 13 Paul describes how the confirming gifts of tongues, prophecy, and knowledge – gifts whereby

---

[32] Kevin DeYoung, "Theological Primer: The 144,000," The Gospel Coalition, April 28, 2017, viewed at https://www.thegospelcoalition.org/blogs/kevin-deyoung/theological-primer-the-144000/.

[33] Ibid.

[34] Ibid.

[35] Mt 16:28-17:2; 2 Pet 1:16-18.

[36] 2 Pet 1:19-21.

[37] 2 Pet 1:21.

[38] E.g., Heb 1:1.

[39] 2 Tim 3:16-17.

God spoke to people – would fulfill their purpose and come to a conclusion.

In a context describing the superiority of love,[40] Paul explains that the gift of tongues would cease on its own.[41] Tongues was a gift which enabled people to speak God's word in actual languages that the speaker didn't understand. This is illustrated in Acts 2:9-11, a passage which includes a list of at least sixteen different languages or dialects by which God used the disciples (and those who were with them) to proclaim God's gospel.

This gift served as a sign to unbelievers,[42] to show that God had sent His Holy Spirit.[43] Paul rebuked the Corinthian church for not utilizing the gift properly at times, and challenged them regarding the importance of love. After that commentary in 1 Corinthians, written in about 51 AD, the Bible never mentions the gift of tongues again – not even in the letter Paul wrote to that same church just a few months later. Very early in church history, the gift of tongues had fulfilled its purpose and ceased on its own, just as Paul indicated it would.

Partial prophecy and knowledge,[44] on the other hand, would continue until the *complete* would arrive,[45] at which time the partial – or incomplete – would be ended. Considering the Greek terminology and syntax of 13:9-10, the issue is not that prophecy and knowledge would be fulfilled by the coming of the complete,[46] but rather that partial[47] prophecy and knowledge would be ended by it. The simplest understanding of these comments by Paul, is that there would come a

---

[40] 1 Cor 13:1-13.
[41] 13:8.
[42] 1 Cor 14:22.
[43] Acts 2:36-38, 10:45-46, 19:5-6.
[44] 1 Cor 13:9.
[45] 13:10.
[46] Greek, *to telion*.
[47] Greek, *ek merous*.

time when God's revealing through prophecy and words of knowledge would come to a conclusion – that He would have said all He had to say. It is evident that milestone is achieved at the conclusion of the book of Revelation, when Jesus leaves the reader expecting no further communication from God, and with only the remaining exception of the two prophets of Revelation 11, until the return of Christ.[48]

Hebrews 1:1-2 tells us that while God used many methods in former times to communicate, in these last days, He "has spoken to us in His Son." Jesus prepared His disciples for His ascension, telling them the Holy Spirit would come to guide them into all the truth.[49] Upon His departure, He reminded them to "make disciples…teaching them to observe all that I commanded you."[50] The Holy Spirit fulfilled that ministry of guiding the disciples into all the truth, as Peter says, "men moved by the Holy Spirit spoke from God."[51] From a textually verifiable standpoint, Jesus' communication, through the Holy Spirit to His disciples, was finished at the end of the book of Revelation. If the closed canon provides clarity regarding the source of authority (God as revealed in the Bible) in a Biblical worldview, then the opening narrative provided in that canon models a hermeneutic pattern for how we should understand Scripture.

THE HERMENEUTIC PRECEDENT OF GENESIS AND JOB

In order to arrive at a *reliable and predictable approach* for interpreting Scriptures, the interpretive method ought to be exegetically derived from within the Scriptural text. Otherwise, there can be no claim to hermeneutic certainty, because any externally derived interpretive method

---

[48] Rev 22:18-20.
[49] Jn 16:13-14.
[50] Mt 28:20.
[51] 2 Pet 1:21.

can be preferred and applied simply by exerting presuppositions upon the text. In the case of an externally derived hermeneutic, presuppositions leading to that hermeneutic conclusion create a pre-understanding that predetermines meaning independent of the author's intentions. The outcome, in such a case, can be wildly different than what the author had in mind.

If the Bible is merely a collection of ancient stories, legends, and myth, interspersed with mildly historical accounts, then the stakes are not particularly high. The greatest damage we can inflict by a faulty hermeneutic method is of the same weight as misunderstanding the motivations and activities of Mark Twain's adventurous character, *Tom Sawyer*, for example. In such an instance we would simply fail to recognize the aesthetic virtues of a creative work. However, if the Bible constitutes an actual revelation from God, then it bears the very authority of the Author, Himself – an authority that extends to every aspect of life and conduct. These are high stakes, indeed. If we fail to engage the text with the interpretive approach intended by its Author, then we fail not just to appreciate aesthetic qualities, but we fail to grasp who God is, and what He intends for us to do.

It is incumbent, then, upon readers of the text to carefully derive hermeneutic method from the Scriptures themselves. Yet, this responsibility is complicated by an obvious absence of prescriptive material within the Biblical text that if present could direct readers toward a particular interpretive stance. In the absence of such prescriptive material, we examine here some descriptive elements from the book of Genesis, in order to discover whether or not there is actually a prevailing hermeneutic embedded in the text itself.

From the opening of Genesis to its conclusion, the book records roughly two thousand years of history. Further, Genesis alleges that these two thousand years are the *first years* of human history.[52] Within that framework of chronology, the events in the book of Genesis account for the first 33% of our recorded six thousand year history and the first 50% of the four thousand years of Biblical history. *If Genesis were univocal regarding hermeneutic method,* that single voice would go a long way in helping us understand how the Author intended for us to interpret the Scriptures. Genesis would be a guiding light, providing the time-tested descriptive model foundational to our Scriptural hermeneutics.

In order to assess the hermeneutic method applied *within Genesis, during the times which the book describes,* we simply examine in Genesis the occurrences of God speaking and the responses of those who heard. The questions addressed here include whether or not God's initial audiences took Him *only* literally or whether they instead or additionally perceived that He intended a deeper meaning than what would be normally signified by the words that were verbally expressed. The responses are categorized as follows: Category 1 (C1) responses are those providing evidence that the initial speech act was intended for literal understanding only; category 2 (C2) responses are those providing evidence that the initial speech act was intended for any understanding beyond the literal meaning of the words verbally expressed. In eighty-four passages in Genesis, we observe at least seventy-one C1's and not a single C2.[53]

Other than the eighty-four verses in Genesis evidencing a model for interpreting Scripture, there are ten similar passages in Job that provide a secondary support to the monolithic hermeneutic method evident thus far in Genesis. In each instance of Divine speech acts in Job, the speaker is identified as "the Lord."[54] In these ten verses, we find ten C1's and zero C2's. Notably, one of the C1 responses is from God,

[52] C.f., Gen 1:27 and 5:1.
[53] Christopher Cone, *Priority in Biblical Hermeneutics and Theological Method* (Raymore, MO: Exegetica Publishing, 2017), 17-36.
[54] Heb. *Yahweh.*

Himself.[55] Job's record of God's speech acts and the responses indicates there is no deviation from the pattern modeled in Genesis. Further, Job's response to God's use of metaphorical language in chapters 40-41 indicates that the Divine use of figurative language did not change the expectation that what was verbally expressed should be interpreted in a basic, face-value, common-sense way. In short, the addition of figurative language did not result in any adjustment to the hermeneutic method.

In examination of the ninety-four passages in Genesis and Job that record Divine speech acts, the evidence is overwhelming (*eighty-one C1's to absolutely zero C2's*) that God intended for His words to be taken at face value, using a plain-sense interpretive approach. The hermeneutic method that reflects this straightforward methodology has become known as the *literal grammatical historical hermeneutic*. This method recognizes that verbal expression has meaning rooted in and inseparable from the grammatical and historical context of the language used, and that these components require that readers be consistent in applying the interpretive method in their study of the Scriptures.

Because of the two-thousand-year precedent evident in Genesis and Job, any departure from the simplicity of this method bears a strong exegetical burden of proof, requiring that there be *explicit exegetical support for any change one might perceive as necessary in handling later Scriptures*. Absent any such exegetical data, we can conclude that (1) hermeneutic methodology for understanding Scripture is not arbitrary but is instead plainly modeled, and that (2) later Scriptures should be understood in light of the hermeneutic precedent provided by Genesis and Job.

---

[55] Job 40:6.

EXTRA-BIBLICAL MATERIAL IN TRANSFORMATIVE
TEACHING AND LEARNING

Paul describes transformation as a process occurring in the life of all believers (even the immature Corinthians).[56] He prescribes that the believer be active in this process of transformation through the renewing of the mind.[57] Transformative learning, from Paul's description and prescription, would simply be *the renewing of the mind*, and would not be merely a mental thing, but also one that involves the spirit.[58] It would involve putting aside the old man, with respect to its manner of conduct,[59] and putting on the new man,[60] which is designed for good conduct.[61] For Paul, then, transformation involves *a mental process that effects the spirit, engages the will, and is manifested in conduct*. This transformative renewal is designed to be a practical outworking of the position reality of what was accomplished by the Holy Spirit in believers at the completed work of their positional salvation (justification).[62]

While not addressing spiritual implications of education and learning, Jack Mezirow observes that *meaning* is often absent in learning models. He suggests, "There is need for a learning theory that can explain how adult learners make sense or meaning of their experiences...These understandings must be explained in the context of adult development and social goals."[63] Mezirow does recognize that learning should be more than a mental process, and that there must be some context and purpose for the learning if it is to be impactful and transformative. He further

---

[56] 2 Corinthians 3:18.

[57] Romans 12:2.

[58] Ephesians 4:23.

[59] Ephesians 4:22.

[60] Ephesians 4:24.

[61] Ephesians 2:10.

[62] Titus 3:5.

[63] Jack Mezirow, *Transformative Dimensions of Adult Learning* (San Francisco, CA:Jossey-Bass, 1991), xii.

noted that a learning theory centered on meaning could provide a firm philosophical foundation for goal setting, needs assessment, program development, instruction, and research.[64] For Mezirow, this theory of transformative learning suggests a robust pedagogy for change. He recognizes the role of hermeneutics in the learning process – implying that learners must be able to effectively exegete their experience in order to achieve their desired outcomes. Mezirow observes, "it is not so much what happens to people but how they interpret and explain what happens to them that determines their actions, their hopes, their contentment and emotional well-being, and their performance."[65] Appropriate interpretation and explanation are necessary for transformation to take place.

Beyond that, "All transformative learning involves taking action to implement insights derived from critical reflection."[66] For Mezirow, transformation is first hermeneutic, then practical. Despite his inattention to the Biblical roots of transformative learning, he has brought to the forefront a theory of learning that is more holistic than the (Friere-coined) deposit method of learning, and in its more comprehensive impact on the person, comes closer in scope to a Biblical model of learning. Consequently, this writer uses the term transformative learning (which Mezirow popularized), to refer to the holistic learning process described and prescribed in Scripture, and not to refer directly to Mezirow's ideas, though there are similarities in the two learning frameworks.

Three Categories of Extra-Biblical Resources and Their Degree of Complementarity in the Transformative Process

In B+T, extra-biblical materials are often perceived as divinely authorized and animated to cooperate with Scripture. Some of these

---

[64] Ibid.
[65] Ibid., xiii.
[66] Ibid., 225.

include the Tradition of the church, the bread and wine of Eucharist in transubstantiation, and the Pope's *ex cathedra* proclamations. These do not merely facilitate a setting in which transformation can occur, but rather they are a necessary part – *co-equal with Scripture* – in transformation. In B+t, some extra-biblical materials are used *as the lens through which to view Scripture*, and thus as a hermeneutic device for undergirding transformative learning. While theoretically these hermeneutic keys are not attributed divine authority, in practice they are given the weight of the divine. However, in the B+∅ approach, the Bible is the exclusive source of authority as God's revelation. While Christ is, Himself, both the revealed God and the revelation of God, the Bible is His commissioned work to record His instructions for those who would have transformed lives, and the text provides its own hermeneutic principles for the reader's understanding. Still, even within Biblical contexts it is evident that extra-revelatory resources can legitimately function in complementary roles, helping to provide a setting for transformative learning.

Experiences in General (2 Timothy 3:10-11)

　　Paul reminded Timothy of the value not only of Paul's teaching, but also of his conduct, purpose, faith patience, love, perseverance, persecutions, and suffering. While he never implies that these bear any revelatory authority, Paul cites particular happenings that Timothy observed, and evokes illustrations in Timothy's memory of Paul's exhibiting the fruits of transformation in those events. Illustration and remembrance are part of Paul's pedagogy in training Timothy. They are not, in themselves, the content that Timothy needs to be passing along,[67] but they are tools that Paul uses to help Timothy contextualize that content.

---

[67] 2 Timothy 2:2.

Bread and Resources for Sustenance (Matthew 4:4, Deuteronomy 8:3)

During His temptation at the hands of Satan, Jesus responded by quoting Deuteronomy 8:3, reminding readers that God had provided bread (manna) to His people, but that bread was not the source of their sustenance, God was. This was an important lesson that even when we lack physical sustenance, we can remain confident in Him, for He has provided His word – that which equips us. The believer's strength and hope, then, is not found in physical provision, but in reliance upon Him based on what He has said. This event was a vivid illustration of the sufficiency of God's word. Still, there was value placed on the physical sustenance. God did, after all, provide manna for the people of Israel. He does indeed understand the physical needs of the people He created.[68]

The challenge Jesus explains in Matthew 6 is the exclusivity of authority. One cannot serve two masters.[69] In the same way, I believe it is an appropriate application of that principle to say that we cannot hold to the authority of His word, while also pursuing another resource as an equal authority. We must serve one or the other. At the same time, while Jesus critiques the pursuit of money, He recognizes that it has an appropriate context in life.[70] After all, it is not money that is the root of all sorts of evil – it is the love of money,[71] and the believer's character ought to be free from that love.[72] In the same way, it is not food or drink or clothing that is the problem – it is the idolatry that results when we pursue those things rather than Him.[73] But if these things are used in their appropriate contexts, then they can be very good and useful in helping us achieve the big picture things He intends for us to accomplish.

---

[68] Matthew 6:30.

[69] 6:24.

[70] Matthew 25:27.

[71] 1 Timothy 6:10.

[72] Hebrews 13:5.

[73] E.g., Mark 7:19, Acts 10:11-15, 1 Corinthians 6:13, 1 Timothy 5:23.

Helps Beyond Scripture (Matthew 4:11)

At the conclusion of Jesus' temptation, angels ministered to Him. This is a remarkable happening, and one that is not presented in detail. Still, it is evident that Jesus had declined Satan's aid, instead focusing on the Scriptures as the way through the temptation. The angelic help that was present afterward seems an affirmation that God indeed understands the importance of physical needs, and has designed that those who would follow Him – as Christ exemplified – should consider their physical needs as secondary in priority to the need to understand and properly apply God's word.

There are other similar instances in which extra-biblical helps are offered. James suggests that when one is struggling and is sick, prayer of the elders should be accompanied by an anointing of oil.[74] There seems an acknowledgment that medicinal aids should not be ignored, but do play a role. Paul doesn't send Timothy to Scripture nor does he encourage Timothy to pray about his stomach challenges – Paul tells Timothy to drink some wine.[75] Paul also challenges Timothy to understand that while godliness is valuable for everything, physical exercise is worth little. Not nothing – but little.[76] God didn't teleport Jonah to the shore (like he seemingly teleported Philip to an evangelistic appointment[77]), he used a sea-creature to carry Jonah to shore.[78] Jesus didn't simply miraculously fill the stomachs of the thousands who were hungry, he used some bread and fish as a key ingredient of His miracle.[79] Jesus didn't simply levitate or fly across the water, rather He chose to walk *on* it.[80] These are just a few of

---

[74] James 5:13.
[75] 1 Timothy 5:23.
[76] 1 Timothy 4:8.
[77] Acts 8:39-40.
[78] Jonah 1:17, 2:10.
[79] John 6:1-14.
[80] Matthew 14:25.

many, many examples of how God chose to employ His physical creation to complement or provide a context for the application of His word.

Consequently, it would not seem shocking that while we should not value those extra-biblical aspects at the level we value His word, there is still value found in them. B+T would value them as equally necessary. B+t would value the extra-biblical as a hermeneutical aid. B+Ø would value them only insofar as the literal grammatical-historical hermeneutic will allow.

CASE STUDY:
APPLICATIONS OF EXTRA-BIBLICAL RESOURCES
IN PSYCHOLOGY AND COUNSELING

Paul encourages transformative learning in several contexts in 1 Thessalonians. In 2:11-12 he describes "exhorting (*parakalountes*), encouraging (*paramuthoumenoi*), and imploring (*marturomenoi*)" believers to walk appropriately. These three are modes of communication for facilitating transformation through mental processes that effect the spirit, engage the will, and are manifested in conduct – the believer's walk. In 5:14-15 Paul exhorts (*parakaloumen*)[81] believers to engage with one another in several particular ways: admonish (*noutheteite*) the unruly, encourage (*paramutheisthe*) the fainthearted, help (*antechesthe*) the weak, be patient (*makrothumeite*) with all, see (*orate*) that no one repays evil for evil, and pursue (*diokete*) good for one another and for all.

These six imperatives are indicative of speech and action that is helpful for the growth of believers. Three of them could be considered forms of Biblical counseling (admonishing, encouraging, helping),[82] one describes the manner in which that counseling is done (with patience),

---

[81] Using the same verb as in 2:11.
[82] Of course, these are not the only forms of Biblical counseling, but they do seem to exemplify essential techniques of a Biblical approach to transformative learning.

and the remaining two pertain to outcomes of Biblical counseling (seeing that no one responds to evil with evil, and pursuing the good). While we don't find the term "counseling" used in the NT, exactly, if we are using the term to describe believers' admonishing, encouraging, and helping of other believers, then we can see a ready correlation between transformative teaching/learning and a Biblical approach to counseling. Further, Paul's exhortation does not seem to limit the scope of benefit to only believers – he urges believers to always be pursuing the good of one another *and* everyone. He seems to distinguish between believers (one another) and unbelievers everyone else). It is evident from these passages that a Biblical approach to counseling for transformation would be focused on believers but could also extend to unbelievers. Beyond the scope of counseling as including believers and unbelievers it is helpful to understand the prescribed tools for counseling, and how the three perspectives (B+T, B+t, and B+Ø) might define and apply the tools.

B+T: One Common Method, Two Disparate Conclusions

As the fundamental principle of B+T is the equality of the Bible and Tradition, there are two iterations of B+T that are discernible here, both sharing a presuppositional methodology.[83] One would be that of the RCC (this approach will be distinguished hereafter by the label B+T/RCC), and the other would represent those who equate the Bible and popular findings that are considered to be scientific (hereafter referred to as B+T/PSP, for popular scientific perspective).

The B+T/RCC approach is well illustrated by Pope Pius XII. He first acknowledges the distinct metaphysical conclusions of the RCC and secular humanist perspectives:

---

[83] That is to say that both work from the same presupposition that the Bible and Tradition (or the doctrines of the field) have essentially equal authority.

Man is entirely the work of the Creator. Even though psychology does not take this into account in its researches, in its experiments and clinical applications, it is always on the work of the Creator that it labors; this consideration is essential from the religious and moral point of view, but as long as the theologian and the psychologist remain objective, no conflict need be feared, and both can proceed in their own fields according to the principles of their science.[84]

Further, he affirms the value of the science of psychology, noting that, "Tests and other psychological methods of investigation have contributed enormously to the knowledge of the human personality and have been of considerable service to it."[85] At the same time he recognizes there are limits to the authority that psychology possesses. He asserts that "Moral law teaches that scientific demands do not by themselves alone justify the indiscriminate use of psychological techniques and methods, even by serious psychologists and for useful objectives."[86] Psychological methodology is subject to moral law (which is derived by nature, revelation, and reason all working in concert). To solidify that point, Pius adds,

Psychology as a science can only make its demands prevail insofar as the echelon of values and higher norms to which We have referred and which includes right, justice equity, respect of human dignity, and well ordered charity for oneself and for others, is respected. There is nothing mysterious in these norms. They are clear for any honest conscience and are formulated by natural

---

[84] Pope Pius XII, "Applied Psychology" addressed to the Rome Congress of the International Association of Applied Psychology, April 10, 1958, I3a, viewed at https://www.ewtn.com/library/PAPALDOC/P12APPSY.HTM.

[85] Ibid., II.

[86] Ibid, II1.

reasoning and by Revelation. Inasmuch as they are observed, there is nothing to prevent the just demands of the science of psychology in favor of modern methods of investigation from being asserted.[87]

While these papal assertions correctly subject psychology to theistic metaphysics and to moral law, the metaphysics and morals are still co-written by Text and Tradition. This allows room for equal input from the discipline or the science, along with the Text and the Tradition. Michael Horne, Catholic Charities Director of Clinical Services, identifies a distinctiveness of Catholic counseling found in the striving "to integrate the Catholic faith into all our services."[88] Catholic Therapist, John Chavez, also advocates an integrative approach, observing that,

> ...most clinical psychologists favor a traditional approach to treatment relying on their particular theoretical orientations...Many of these orientations have proven to be effective both for mental illness and daily life problems...However, as a Catholic clinical psychologist, I have not found it always helpful to rely exclusively on traditional methods of therapy. Instead I have found that using both traditional and Catholic-based approaches to therapy are much more effective.[89]

The B+T/RCC approach is integrationist in the sense that Catholic therapists "employ the same empirically-supported psychotherapeutic

---

[87] Ibid.

[88] Michael Horne, "Catholic Counseling and What Makes Us Different" Arlington Catholic Charities, June, 29, 2016, viewed at http://arlingtoncatholiccharities.com/1131-2/.

[89] John Chavez, "Catholic-Based Psychotherapy" CatholicTherapists.com, viewed at https://www.catholictherapists.com/articles/catholic-based-psychotherapy-341.

techniques as mainstream psychotherapy,"[90] as long as they don't directly contradict the tenets of Text and Tradition.

The B+T/PSP approach, on the other hand, borrows from secular humanism in some key areas, and also deviates in some foundational aspects. Where secular humanism attempts consistency in applying worldview to a discipline, is transparent in its denial of God and spiritual things, and gambles everything on the naturalistic premise and the resulting biopsychosocial model, B+T/PSP holds to the existence of God and the supernatural, and ultimately dispenses with consistency in favor of an appealing middle ground. B+T/PSP subjects all but God's existence (and the idea that God revealed Himself) to popular scientific standards, thus perceiving many theological conclusions through the lens of repeatability and provability. More than a few of these conclusions are compatible with materialistic rather than Biblically theistic thinking. Consequently, prescriptions are rooted in materialistic-friendly descriptions. In B+T/PSP thought, there is little to dislike of contemporary mainstream psychology beside the basic anti-supernatural premise. The problem here is that the premise simply invalidates the Bible in its entirety. I refer to this as *The Oil and Water Problem* – if presuppositions and methods don't align, how can the conclusions possibly be expected to align?

B+t: The Hopeful Middle Ground

Clinical Psychologist Sarah Rainer illustrates the hopeful middle ground of the B+t approach. It is notably integrationist, and virtually identical to B+T/RCC. She recognizes that,

---

[90] Ryan Howes, "The Varieties of Religious Therapy: Catholicism: Psychology According to Catholic Scholars," *Psychology Today*, Sept. 21, 2011, viewed at https://www.psychologytoday.com/us/blog/in-therapy/201109/the-varieties-religious-therapy-catholicism.

The intricacies of the human brain, the environmental influences on our personality, and the social and culture impact on our lives remind me that pathology cannot simply be reduced to issues of morality or sin. On the other hand, as a Christian, I acknowledge that all humans are inherently separated from God. This separation causes disorder, sin, and disease of every kind… I propose that Christian mental health professionals operate on a middle ground, the bio/psycho/social/spiritual model, which considers both our dignity and depravity as humans.[91]

At first glance this middle ground looks and sounds like B+T, in that mental and environmental issues seem to share equal prominence with sin and depravity. However, she does clarify an order of priority: "The use of some secular therapy interventions is not inherently wrong; the overreliance and/or independent use of these techniques is… When research and Christianity contradict each other, we follow the latter."[92] But while asserting the superiority of the "B" over the "t," the model that Rainer proposes seems to contradict that assertion. Whereas secular humanism operates on a biopsychosocial model, Rainer proposes a bio/psycho/social/spiritual one. The spiritual component is segregated, and it is last. This model seems to simply add a component to the biopsychosocial model, rather than to recognize that the Bible presents humanity as a spiritual being who possesses the other traits.[93] This is the tension evident within an integrationist approach. It does attempt to utilize all sources of knowledge, but has difficulty in prioritizing. It

---

[91] Sarah Rainer, "The Integration of Psychology and Christianity: A Guest Post by Sarah Rainer," *Christianity Today*, Sept. 25, 2014, viewed at https://www.christianitytoday.com/edstetzer/2014/september/concerning-psychology-and-christianity-guest-post-by-sarah-.html.

[92] Ibid.

[93] Genesis 2:7, Adam became a living soul (*nephesh*), In Job 7:11, Job possesses both spirit (*ruach*) and soul (*nephesh*).

chooses the Bible when there are clear contradictions, but may not prioritize the Bible when there are not contradictions (e.g., bio/psycho/social/spiritual model).

It also seems to underemphasize Biblical training. If the spiritual issues are equally as important as the other issues, then shouldn't a therapist have an equal amount of training in understanding the Biblical metaphysic and all of what that implies? Other issues worthy of further investigation here are the superimposing of brain and mind illness, definitions in pathology, and perspectives on the environment and culture as non-moral. Once again, the Oil and Water Problem seem to be in view.

Christian Psychology

To resolve some of these integrative tensions, some within the B+t community have advocated a "Christian Psychology" application, which develops a separate stream of psychology science within the Christian faith tradition. It does this by establishing and relying on validity of instruments within the tradition itself: methodology is a combination of conceptual historical and empirical research. It asserts that the "Foundational commitment of Jesus' psychology is to love (unconditional positive regard),"[94] that research supports the idea that praying and meditative communion with God has beneficial effects,[95] and that "Christian beliefs about sin and about grace broadly predict better psychological adjustment."[96] This brand of Christian Psychology is focused not on deconstruction of secular theories but construction of its own. Roberts adds, "If a psychology is at heart an ethical system, an ideal of human functioning with corollary ideas about what's wrong with people and how they can move from dysfunction to better function, then

---

[94] Robert Roberts and Paul Watson, "Christian Psychology," October 17, 2013, viewed at https://prezi.com/96xraoi3vjja/christian-psychology-robert-c-roberts-paul-j-watson/?webgl=0).

[95] Ibid.

[96] Ibid.

Christianity has always been in the psychology business, and should take its proper place among the various psychologies that are being offered today."[97] Roberts finds it troubling that if psychology is scientific at its core, then there should not be a diversity of modern psychologies. He notes that, "we do not see eight or ten rival chemistries all operating in the same decade so that the student has to study them and choose which one he likes best."[98] Roberts observes that "Physics and chemistry are scientific at their conceptual core, while psychologies—at least the kind that we call personality theories and clinical models—are scientific on the periphery."[99] If psychology is only peripherally scientific, then, "every psychology is at its core an ethical-spiritual conceptual system that is less than fully dictated by mere observations of human beings,"[100] and "when we study psychology we are always studying "ideology."[101] While this approach has the advantages of understanding that psychology is not in itself a hard science[102] and it engages in research to positively construct a Christian psychology, the familiar disadvantages limit the potential of this approach: tradition and historical perspectives (historical theology) are elevated to prescriptive status, and this model is more focused on a "Christian" rather than Biblical psychology and worldview.

---

[97] Robert Roberts, "Redeeming Psychology Means Recovering the Christian Psychology of the Past," *Responding*, June 1, 2009, viewed at
https://www.cardus.ca/comment/article/redeeming-psychology-means-recovering-the-christian-psychology-of-the-past/.

[98] Ibid.

[99] Ibid.

[100] Ibid.

[101] Ibid.

[102] Though there are certainly physiological scientific factors [e.g., brain science] which it engages.

Nouthetic Counseling

Another B+t approach that has become popular in the last thirty years is Nouthetic Counseling. Jay Adams introduces this system that he pioneered:

> "While the name is new, the sort of counseling done by nouthetic counselors is not. From Biblical times onward, God's people have counseled nouthetically. The word itself is Biblical. It comes from the Greek noun *nouthesia* (verb: *noutheteo*). The word, used in the New Testament primarily by the apostle Paul, is translated "admonish, correct or instruct." This term, which probably best describes Biblical counseling, occurs in such passages as Romans 15:14: I myself am convinced about you, my brothers, that you yourselves are full of goodness, filled with all knowledge, and competent to counsel one another…The three ideas found in the word nouthesia are confrontation, concern, and change…To put it simply, *nouthetic counseling consists of lovingly confronting people out of deep concern in order to help them make those changes that God requires.*[103]

Adams' description of Nouthetic methodology is distinctive, and worth repeating here:

> By confrontation we mean that one Christian personally gives counsel to another from the Scriptures. He does not confront him with his own ideas or the ideas of others. He limits his counsel strictly to that which may be found in the Bible, believing that "*All Scripture is breathed out by God and useful for teaching, for conviction, for correction and for disciplined training in righteousness in order to fit and fully equip the man from God for every good task.*" (2 Timothy 3:16,17)…The

---

[103] Jay Adams, "What is "Nouthetic" Counseling?" Institute for Nouthetic Studies, viewed at http://www.nouthetic.org/about-ins/what-is-nouthetic-counseling.

nouthetic counselor believes that all that is needed to help another person love God and his neighbor as he should, as the verse above indicates, may be found in the Bible....By concern we mean that counseling is always done for the benefit of the counselee. His welfare is always in view in Biblical counseling. The apostle Paul put it this way: "I am not writing these things to shame you, but to counsel you as my dear children" (1 Corinthians 4:14)... Plainly, the familial nature of the word *noutheteo* appears in this verse. There is always a warm, family note to biblical counseling which is done among the saints of God who seek to help one another become more like Christ...Christians consider their counseling to be a part of the sanctification process whereby one Christian helps another get through some difficulty that is hindering him from moving forward in his spiritual growth...By change we mean that counseling is done because there is something in another Christian's life that fails to meet the biblical requirements and that, therefore, keeps him from honoring God...All counseling—Biblical or otherwise—attempts change.[104]

Adams emphasize that only Biblical counselors know what a counselee should become, and that the result of counseling should be that the counselee should look more like Christ.[105] Even though Adams' approach is decidedly behavioristic, he does acknowledge that it is God who makes the changes in the person "as His word is ministered in the power of the Spirit."[106]

The greatest advantage of the Nouthetic approach is that it truly attempts to exalt the sufficiency of Scripture. Further, it rejects

---

[104] Ibid.
[105] Ibid.
[106] Ibid.

mainstream, integrated, and Christian psychology. However, there are some significant disadvantages: Nouthetic is imbalanced, in that all counseling is considered to be admonishment; it is very behavioristic and sin focused; It abandons the discipline of psychology altogether; it is rooted in the B+t of contemporary Reformed or Covenant theology. Each of these concerns is significant enough to warrant discussion here.\

Problem #1: Admonishment ≠ All Counseling

In a Venn diagram illustrating this assertion, the two circles would be completely overlapping (Diagram A.), but this doesn't square with the Biblical data. There are eleven NT instances of νουθετέω/νουθεσία. Five are descriptive.[107] Six of these instances are prescriptive,[108] and in several of these νουθετέω/νουθεσία is considered *with other verbs*, so there is no exegetical warrant for asserting that all counseling is simply nouthetic.

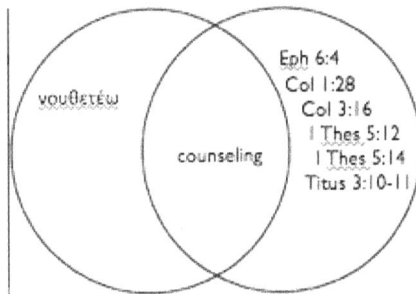

Diagram A.   Diagram B.

---

[107] Acts 20:31-32 (admonish and commend), Romans 15:14, 1 Corinthians 4:14, 10:11, and 2 Thessalonians 3:15.

[108] Ephesians 6:4, Colossians 1:28, 3:16, 1 Thessalonians 5:12, 5:14, and Titus 3:10.

Problem #2: The Behavioristic Sin Focus

Notice the emphasis on works as separate from and *preceding* honoring God: "By change we mean that counseling is done because there is something in another Christian's life that fails to meet the biblical requirements and that, therefore, keeps him from honoring God."[109] Again, we have an exegetical problem. Note that Job was not guilty of sin, but ignorance.[110] Further, we are told to reject a factious man after a first and second warning, knowing that such a man is perverted and is sinning, being self-condemned,[111] whereas a wise man will hear and increase in learning, and a man of understanding will acquire wise counsel.[112] In other words, it is the wise man who increases in learning, and his increase is not connected to the eradication of sin behaviors, but rather to a process of (transformative) learning.

Problem #3: Abandons the Discipline of Psychology

Psychology is not a worldview, it is a discipline or field of study, and more specifically, it is the study of the mind, soul. While all perspectives on psychology are grounded in worldview, there is one worldview perspective that is correct: who knows the mind and soul better than the Creator? The Bible is the authoritative source for knowledge of the mind and soul, thus the primary textbook for proper psychology (Biblical psychology). There are truths outside of the Bible in many disciplines that we find useful (logic, math, physics, propositional truths, descriptions, etc.). These are extra-biblical, subject to Scripture, and still useful. They are not to be equated (integrated) with, but to be interpreted by the authority of Scripture. Adams understands the challenge:

---

[109] Adams, "What is "Nouthetic" Counseling?"
[110] Job 1:22, 2:10, 40:3-5, 42:1-6.
[111] Titus 3:10-11.
[112] Proverbs 1:5.

"In my understanding, attempted integration of the Scriptures with worldly counseling beliefs, methods, and/or techniques inevitably means that in order to make them agree, the Scriptures are bent to fit the non-scriptural material that the counselor attempts to integrate with it. I believe the task is impossible without ending in a non-scriptural method."[113]

However, by throwing out the entire discipline of psychology, the consequence is that Christians have abandoned the study of the mind and the soul to those who deny the Creator. Christians have doomed an entire field of study to be populated by falsehood.

Problem #4: Built on a Covenant Platform

This problem is discernible in three specific ways. First, the B+t approach is evident in the methodology of Reformed/Covenant theology: begin with theology and exegete in light of that (incidentally, that is eerily similar to the RCC hermeneutic). DeYoung teaches that "Your theological system should tell you how to exegete."[114] Adams is transparent about how theological pre-commitments impact his interpretation:

If a matter has been settled by the church, it is wrong to stir up the thinking of the general population of Christians about any change in such long-settled theology unless it is clearly an exegetically-supported change that can be demonstrated to be a

---

113 Jay Adams, "Competent to Counsel: An Interview With Jay Adams," Ligonier Ministries, Feb 1, 2014, viewed at
https://www.ligonier.org/learn/articles/competent-counsel-interview-jay-adams/.
114 DeYoung "Your Theological System Should Tell You How to Exegete."

genuine advance in thought that improves upon accepted Reformation doctrine.[115]

A second problematic aspect of the Nouthetic counseling approach is that the limited atonement view (which Adams asserts is central to the theology that undergirds Nouthetic counseling) makes it impossible to counsel an unbeliever that Jesus died for them.[116] Adams remarks,

> As a reformed Christian, the writer believes that counselors must not tell any unsaved counselee that Christ died for him, for they cannot say that. No man knows except Christ himself who are his elect for whom he died.[117]

A third problem is the mixed message on sanctification, that godliness comes through self-discipline, and sanctification by works of the Law. Adams illustrates this tension, saying,

> Discipline is the secret of godliness...You must learn to discipline yourself for the purpose of godliness... discipline means work; it means sustained daily effort....An athlete becomes an expert only by years of hard practice...[Taking up the cross] means putting to death the old life patterns of the old man....This is what it means to discipline oneself for godliness. It means to continue to say 'no' to self and to say 'yes' to Christ every day until one by one all of the old habitual ways are replaced by new ones. It means that by

---

[115] Jay Adams, "If You Love Me, Keep My Commandments," Institute For Nouthetic Studies, Sept. 30, 2011, viewed at http://www.nouthetic.org/blog/?p=5169.

[116] Christopher Cone, "Culinary Calvinism: Considering Jay Adams' Tulipburger," August 7, 2017, viewed at http://www.drcone.com/2017/08/07/culinary-calvinism-considering-jay-adams-tulipburger/.

[117] Jay Adams, "Evangelism and Counseling," *Competent to Counsel: Introduction to Nouthetic Counseling, EPub Edition* (Grand Rapids, MI: Zondervan, 2009).

daily endeavor to follow God's Son, one finds at length that doing so is more 'natural' than not doing so…If you practice what God tells you to do, the obedient life will become a part of you. There is no simple, quick, easy way to instant godliness.[118]

Paul seems to take a different tact in several passages in his Letter to the Galatians:

This is the only thing I want to find out from you: did you receive the Spirit by the works of the law, or by hearing with faith? Are you so foolish? Having begun by the Spirit are you being perfected by the flesh?[119]

But now that faith has come we are no longer under a tutor.[120]

It was for freedom that Christ set us free; therefore keep standing firm and do not be subject again to a yoke of slavery.[121]

You were running well. Who hindered you from obeying the truth?[122]

But I say walk by the Spirit and you will not carry out the desire of the flesh…But if you are led by the Spirit you are not under the law.[123]

---

[118] Jay Adams, *Godliness Through Discipline* (Philipsburg, NJ: P&R Publishing, 1983), 2,3,5-6.
[119] Galatians 3:2-3.
[120] 3:25.
[121] 5:1.
[122] 5:7.
[123] 5:16-18.

Adams is to be commended for seeking a return to Biblical authority and sufficiency. He made great strides in drawing people to the Scriptures to find their solutions. However, as is the case in any reformation, there often remains the residue of the old and faulty, even as there is an attempt to refine. The intention here is not to castigate Adams, but rather to challenge us to refine, understanding the work Adams has done, deconstruct our understanding of psychology and counseling, and rebuild it not on B+t, but on B+Ø.

B+Ø Applied to Psychology and Counseling

Paul challenges the Colossians to be sure that no one takes them "captive through the philosophy and empty deception, according to the tradition of men, according to the elementary principles of the world, rather than according to Christ."[124] It is important to note that this is not a blanket condemnation of philosophy, but rather an indictment of *the* philosophy that is according to things other than Christ. It is *that kind* of philosophy that captures and enslaves. On the other hand, Paul is desiring that the Colossians would have a correct philosophy – one that is according to Christ. That philosophy is rooted in a proper mindset,[125] and based on the doctrinal and practical elements discussed in Paul's Letter to the Colossians, it could be described as *a mental posture that effects the spirit, engages the will, and is manifested in conduct.* In other words, Paul is advocating the right kind of philosophy, which we could say is the product of transformative learning, and we could add that Biblical counseling could play a significant role in that process, because of the content Paul provides to help us understand what Biblical counseling would look like.

But Biblical counseling is a practical outworking – a prescriptive activity – based on descriptions found in the Bible. In a worldview context, the prescriptive requires a descriptive – there ought to be an *is*

---

[124] Colossians 2:8.
[125] 3:1-4.

upon which the *ought* relies. That descriptive *is* can be understood as the Biblical teaching on metaphysics (the nature of reality) as it pertains to what a person is, what a person needs, and how a person can get what they need. This is within a subset of metaphysics called anthropology, and is a subset of anthropology, that we could call psychology – the study of the human soul or mind. It is that Biblical teaching on these aspects of personhood that should govern our prescriptions toward transformative teaching and learning.

Now, some perceive psychology as a humanistic system of teaching that denies the Creator and operates from the vantage point that humanity is merely matter and energy. But that is not *psychology*. That would be a secular humanistic psychology. Psychology is itself a discipline – nothing more than a field of study. It is not a worldview. But in our times the discipline of psychology has been so overrun by the worldview of secular humanism, that it seems impossible to extricate the discipline from the philosophies that are not according to Christ. Our job is to understand where the content for an accurate psychology is derived. How we answer that question will determine the kind of counseling we will be doing, and from what vantage point. Psychology is not an extra-biblical resource. Psychology is simply the component within metaphysics that provides the *is* to ground the *ought*. The bases for the worldview (epistemology as well as other aspects of metaphysics) will ultimately predetermine the tenets of the psychology. Psychology is a discipline that is populated by the foundational principles of the worldview. Thus, while psychology is not a worldview, it is inextricable from the worldview that defines it. It is therefore incumbent upon counselors who seek to be Biblical to have a thoroughgoing Biblical psychology.

From a B+Ø perspective, the tool needed for this type of transformative teaching/learning is clearly and simply Scripture. Paul is clear about the sufficiency of Scripture for the equipping of believers,[126] and for the enlightening of unbelievers.[127] Undoubtedly, *there is no need for extra-biblical resources in either of these process*, however, there is also no prohibition, and considering the examples experience, resources for sustenance, and helps employed beyond Scripture, we can see some advantage to the proper utilization of extra-biblical tools. Experiences (in the form of illustration and remembrance, for example), tools of sustenance (including medical aids where needed), and helps beyond Scripture (potentially including models, and methods – including scientific – that are observed through the lens of Scripture) may be employed.

Additionally, B+Ø provides modeling for assessment of when extra-biblical can be most helpfully engaged to complement Biblical content. Paul's Acts 17 evangelistic episode in Athens records one such model. First, in 17:22-23 Paul shows familiarity with Greek culture and an ability to dialogue from within that framework. He appeals to a specific point of cultural ignorance in which to inject gospel truth. Then in 17:28 he invokes a line from Aratus' *Phaenomena*, a popular Greek poem. Paul engages with popular culture to meet the Athenians where they are with the truth of the person and work of Jesus Christ.

In other contexts Paul reminds his readers that "all things are permissible, but not all things edify."[128] He challenges them to think on things that are worthy,[129] and to speak only those things that are effective for meeting the need of the moment and for building up the house.[130] The writer of Hebrews encourages believers to "consider how to stimulate one another to love and good deeds."[131] These are transformative teaching and

---

[126] 2 Timothy 3:16-17.
[127] 2 Timothy 3:15.
[128] 1 Corinthians 10:23.
[129] Philippians 4:8.
[130] Ephesians 4:29.
[131] Hebrews 10:24.

learning activities, and they don't involve integrating a Biblical approach with extra-biblical concepts, but rather undergirding our entire worldview on the words of Scripture.

(Reformed) Biblical counselor, Jeff Forrey summarizes well the distinctiveness of this approach versus the integrative approach:

> Perhaps...we could say there is a need for reinterpretation as Christians consider the claims made by mainstream psychologists. And these two processes are different. "Integration" assumes a *continuity* between secular and biblical worldview presuppositions that cannot be assumed to exist. "Reinterpretation" assumes a *discontinuity* between the two worldviews that requires a different way of understanding concepts or theories in relationship to what the Bible teaches.[132]

I would describe this as infusion versus refraction. Infusion (think of the process of brewing coffee) can be passive and distortive. One ingredient is received by another, resulting in a third product. Biblical thinking can be infused with secular psychology, integrated psychology, even Christian psychology, or Nouthetic psychology. But what we are after is refraction. Refraction can be active and corrective, allowing the observer to observe accurately. The Bible is the refractive lens through which to interpret and reinterpret all knowledge of the mind/soul. And before we can counsel Biblically, we must have an understanding of the Biblical psychology.

This approach has the advantage of seeking to view all knowledge through the lens of Scripture, and to subject all knowledge to the authority of Scripture. It encourages science and research within the field of

---

[132] Jeff Forrey, "A Response to "The Integration of Christianity and Psychology: A Guest Post by Sarah Rainer," Biblical Counseling Coalition, October 27, 2014, viewed at http://biblicalcounselingcoalition.org/2014/10/27/a-response-to-the-integration-of-christianity-and-psychology-a-guest-post-by-sarah-rainer/.

psychology. It offers a Biblical balance of description and prescription. Of course, if the Bible is unreliable, then the refractive power of Scripture is distortive rather than corrective, but the epistemological premise of the B+Ø approach is that God's word is authoritative and sufficient for our understanding, for our equipping, and for our practice. There are many extra-biblical resources that we can employ, but in seeking out how and when to do that, we mustn't lose sight of the one reliable constant that God has provided for us – the Bible.

Recognizing and Applying
Biblical Authority
and Biblical Sufficiency

Adding
Secular Humanism
to the Bible
(Integrationism)

Adding
Tradition
to the Bible
(Integrationism)

Integrating
Secular Humanism
with the Bible (Liberalism)

Integrating Tradition
with the Bible (Legalism)

Complementing
Secular Humanism
with the Bible (Existentialism)

Complementing
Tradition
with the Bible (Pharisaism)

Denying Biblical Authority
and Biblical Sufficiency
(Secularism)

10

Eight Qualities for Counseling Technique

Luther Ray Smith Jr., Psy.D

INTRODUCTION

Counseling is the relational process by which a person instructs and guides another,[1] and takes place when a person obtains wisdom from another person.[2] Counseling can occur informally (e.g., one friend seeking guidance from another friend) and or formally (e.g., a trained counselor with their knowledge and expertise guiding a counselee). The skills and exercises a counselor use to guide the counselees to the goals outlined in counseling are *counseling techniques.*[3]

Those who endorse counseling from a Biblical outlook may with good reason express concern about the methods that a counselor uses. As one author has observed, "the counseling field is restless, fluid, volatile. Fads, fashions, and factions come and go. Theories and therapies

---

[1] This description of counseling in found in the chapter "Psychology: Discipline or Worldview," written by Dr. Luther Smith.
[2] This description of counseling is found in the chapter "Where Can Wisdom Be Found?" written by Dr. Jeffery Cox.
[3] "Technique (n.)." Accessed January 3, 2021. https://www.etymonline.com/word/technique.

shift, mutate, combine, innovate, and reinvent themselves. There's always the next best-seller and the newest sure-fire cure that transcends the limitations of all that came before."[4] It is true one's paradigm *does* impact the approach of the counselor. It is also true that a counselor's worldview may influence the goals of counseling, and the technique a counselor may use within the counseling process. Yet, some counseling techniques, even though they may be promoted by secular counselors, could prove to be helpful. For example, both secular and Biblical counseling approaches utilize the technique of *homework* throughout the counseling process. A Biblical counselor described the advantage of well-crafted homework:

> Homework is more than guided Bible study, reinforcing the teaching aspect of counseling. Homework for the biblical counselor is not limited to a single focus and single purpose. Homework, creatively designed and appropriately used, advances each phase of counseling. Used well, homework doesn't function as an addition to the counseling process but as an integral part of it. Each step of the counseling process continues, even when counselee and counselor are not together, because good homework keeps the movement going.[5]

A counselor who specializes in the Cognitive Behavioral Therapy (CBT) approach, when discussing the importance of homework in the counseling process wrote, "Homework is an important component of

[4] Powlison, David. "What Distinguishes Biblical Counseling from Other Methods?" 9Marks, February
26, 2010. https://www.9marks.org/article/what-distinguishes-biblical-counseling-other-methods/.
[5] Tripp, Paul. "Homework and Biblical Counseling, Part 2." The Journal of Biblical Counseling.
Accessed January 3, 2021. http://8fceb942096fcf9407d2-20c5ff882b477b20529d08a30bc17c49.r85.cf2.rackcdn.com/uploaded/h/0e4585164_1444322773_homework-and-bc-part-2-tripp.pdf.

cognitive behavior therapy (CBT) and other evidence-based treatments for psychological symptoms. Developed collaboratively during therapy sessions, homework assignments may be used by clients to rehearse new skills, practice coping strategies, and restructure destructive beliefs."[6]

Usually techniques employed by the counselor are utilized for the purpose of fulfilling the goals the counselor outlines for the counselee. One result is that the counselee may be confident that the problem they are presenting is being addressed. However, in terms of Biblical counseling, how can a counselor be assured that the techniques they use are aligned with the Biblical worldview? This chapter explores the aspects of humanity, the qualities that humanity possesses, and how these qualities are addressed with counseling technique. We also look at two case studies from Scripture regarding techniques that can be used to address problems regarding the qualities of humanity, and we explore characteristics of counseling techniques.

THE QUALITIES OF HUMANITY UNDERSCORED IN THE BOOK OF GENESIS

The qualities of humanity are highlighted in the book of Genesis. In Genesis 2 it is recorded that God created humanity from the dust of the ground,[7] and animated man by breathing into man's nostrils.[8] From God's activity we observe the substance of humanity – that humanity is *material* (consisting of a physical body and all of the organs that parts that

---

[6] Minden, Joel. "How Much Does Homework Matter in Therapy?" Psychology Today. Sussex
  Publishers, April 16, 2017. https://www.psychologytoday.com/us/blog/cbt-and-me/201704/how-much-
  does-homework-matter-in-therapy.
[7] Genesis 2:7.
[8] Ibid.

are associated with the body).[9] In addition, humanity is *immaterial* – revealed as having a *spirit*.[10] God, After creating man placed him in the garden of Eden to labor among the vegetation.[11] Man (along with woman) was to rule and care for the animals.[12] This quality that is found among humanity is the ability to labor and produce with the resources that God had created.

This emphasized that Adam and Eve had the mental and cognitive capability to complete the necessary work. God created humanity with material and immaterial qualities, and by His grace He has allowed humanity the privilege by our labor to participate in addressing these aspects of humanity according to His word.

CHARACTERISTICS OF COUNSELING TECHNIQUES: A CASE STUDY FROM THE BOOK OF EXODUS

One case study underscoring counseling technique is found in the interaction between Jethro and Moses. While Jethro praised the Lord for rescuing the nation of Israel from the hand of the Egyptians, Moses began to evaluate the people's conflicts and problems for the entire nation of Israel.[13]

> Now when Moses' father-in-law saw all that he was doing for the people, he said, "What is this thing that you are doing for the people? Why do you alone sit as judge and all the people stand about you from morning until evening?" Moses said to his father-in-law, "Because the people come to me to inquire of God. When they have a dispute, it comes to me, and I judge between a man

---

[9] Ibid.
[10] Ibid.
[11] Genesis 2:15.
[12] Genesis 1:26-28.
[13] Exodus 18:13.

and his neighbor and make known the statutes of God and His laws."[14]

Even though the emphasis of the author in this context is not explicitly about counseling techniques, there are qualities of counseling techniques we can glean from this passage The first characteristic evident is *inquiring about the counselee's presenting problem.* Jethro noticed Moses was the only one that was adjudicating disputes within the entire nation of Israel.[15] Jethro noticed the lack of efficiency in this and questioned Moses concerning whether his approach was expedient. Before Jethro gave his counsel to Moses, Jethro observed Moses's activity among the people. Jethro was *intentional* to ask a question concerning Moses's actions so that Jethro would have understanding of the situation.

There is another quality to notice in this passage. Moses seemed convinced his actions in addressing the issues was the best thing he could have done given the situation, even if these actions would produce extreme physical exhaustion. Moses was called by God to deliver the nation of Israel.[16] Moses was also given the responsibility to lead Israel out of Egypt.[17] Jethro recognized that the calling and responsibility did not necessitate Moses's actions. "Moses' father-in-law said to him, "The thing that you are doing is not good. You will surely wear out, both yourself and these people who are with you, for the task is too heavy for you; you cannot do it alone."[18] The second characteristic of counseling technique is *observing the counselee's behavior or the conduct that is ineffective and counterproductive.* After observing and inquiring about Moses, Jethro stated that the quality of Moses's conduct was not helpful or beneficial for himself, nor for the people Moses sought to counsel. Jethro chided Moses

---

[14] Exodus 18:14-16.
[15] Exodus 18:13.
[16] Exodus 3:8-10.
[17] Exodus 3:10.
[18] Exodus 18:17-18.

that the work he was doing all by himself was too great, suggested Moses should find support.

A third characteristic of counseling techniques is also evident in this context:

> Now listen to me: I will give you counsel, and God be with you. You be the people's representative before God, and you bring the disputes to God. then teach them the statutes and the laws and make known to them the way in which they are to walk and the work they are to do. "Furthermore, you shall select out of all the people able men who fear God, men of truth, those who hate dishonest gain; and you shall place these over them as leaders of thousands, of hundreds, of fifties and of tens. Let them judge the people at all times; and let it be that every major dispute they will bring to you, but every minor dispute they themselves will judge. So it will be easier for you, and they will bear the burden with you."[19]

Jethro demonstrates *administering guidance that addresses the counselee's presenting problem explicitly*. In observing the conduct and the consequences, Jethro petitioned Moses to consider his counsel. Jethro advised that Moses ought to instruct others how to adjudicate disputes between the people. Additionally, Jethro was very specific in his guidance for Moses. Moses ought to find men who displayed reverence to the God of Israel and were upstanding people as rulers over certain groups of Israelites. This course of action would help protect Moses from the extreme exhaustion he would otherwise encounter.

A fourth quality of counseling technique modeled here is that it *ought to be instructive to the person receiving the counseling*. The counsel Jethro

---

[19] Exodus 18:19-21.

gave to Moses was *useful* to Moses. Jethro's counsel contained information that was directly related to the problem Moses had in advising the nation of Israel. In communicating his guidance to Moses, Jethro provided specifics. Jethro told Moses *who* ought to be involved in this process (God-fearing truthful men), *how* they should be involved in this process (the division of labor among all those who were chosen), and the *type* of evaluations and disputes these men ought to be responsible for.

The fifth characteristic illustrated in the passage is that *the technique a counselee uses should be practical.* The technique ought to be sensible and realistic in terms of addressing the problem the counselee presents. Because Jethro was detailed in his explanation of how to solve this particular problem, Moses was able to implement this action in his interaction with the people of Israel.[20]

A sixth quality of counseling techniques is that *counseling techniques used by the counselor must correspond to reality.* The techniques used must be grounded in truth. Jethro's counsel corresponded to the processes of the *physical body* (Moses would physically wear himself out) and the *social interactions* between Moses and the people if Israel.

The seventh quality demonstrated in this text is that the *counseling techniques given to the counselee ought to be measurable.* Jethro's counsel coincided with reality, and the results of his advice could be physically observed. Moses implemented the counsel given by Jethro in a way that was documented – hence, measurable.

The last quality of counseling technique evident in this context is that *the counseling techniques ought to be grounded in a proper philosophy and worldview.* This quality is observed in Jethro's answer to Moses when Jethro said, "Now listen to me: I will give you counsel, and God be with you. You be the people's representative before God, and you bring the disputes to God."[21] Jethro explained that the counsel Moses should give

---

[20] Exodus 18:24-27.
[21] Exodus 18:19.

ought to be from the perspective of the wisdom God gave to Moses. Even minor disputes among the people of Israel should be examined in the wisdom that God would provide.[22] Jethro understood that God's wisdom was needed for handling disputes between people.

In offering counsel to Moses in this context, Jethro models eight qualities for counseling technique. It is important that the eight qualities evident here can also be observed in the New Testament.

CHARACTERISTICS OF COUNSELING TECHNIQUES: A CASE STUDY FROM FIRST THESSALONIANS

The eight qualities of counseling techniques can be observed in various New Testament epistles. In Paul's first letter to the churches of Thessalonica he exhorts, "We urge you, brethren, admonish the unruly, encourage the fainthearted, help the weak, be patient with everyone. See that no one repays another with evil for evil, but always seek after that which is good for one another and for all people.[23] Before concluding his letter, Paul offered instruction to the people of Thessalonica. The first quality (*inquiring about the counselee's presenting problem*) is observed within the language of the text. Paul addressed *observable* problems (i.e., unruly, fainthearted, and weak). Paul addressed the conduct where it warranted warning or instruction, comfort, or physical assistance. In that Paul also demonstrated the second quality (*observing the counselee's behavior or the conduct that is ineffective and counterproductive*).

The third characteristic (*administering guidance that addresses the counselee's presenting problem explicitly*) is also embedded in the specific guidance that Paul gave. Paul uses the Greek word νουθετέω (*noutheteo*), the word that translated *admonish*, to address one whose conduct is ἄτακτος (*ataktos*) referring to one who lacks control in their conduct (i.e.,

---

[22] Exodus 18:21-22.
[23] 1 Thessalonians 5:14-15.

"unruly"). Paul wrote that those who are ὀλιγόψυχος (*ogliopyschos*), that is "small souled." Paul used this word to describe a person who lacked strength. Paul told the people of Thessalonica that if one found a person in that situation, the observer should παραμυθέομαι (*paramytheomai*), "encourage" them and give them strength during difficult times. Lastly Paul stated for those who are ἀσθενής (*asthenēs*) – physically disabled and infirmed, that they should be assisted (*antechō*). Paul gave believers in Thessalonica specific words to handle specific problems they were encountering.

The fourth characteristic (*ought to be instructive to the counselee receiving the counseling*) is also evident in this letter. All of the actions Paul described in this letter are *instructive* to the counselees who are receiving the instruction concerning each trouble they face. For those that were unruly they were given instruction with the objective to bring them into right conduct. For individuals who might experience mental and emotional turmoil, they were instructed to take heart as they were guided by His word. For the people in Thessalonica who were ill and disabled they were instructed that they need care and compassion from the those who assist them.

The fifth characteristic of counseling technique (*the technique a counselor uses ought to be practical*) is also found here. Paul offers *action points* for addressing each of the problems he describes – *instruct* those who are unmanageable, *encourage* those who are fainthearted, and *support* those who are ill and disabled.

The sixth quality (*counseling techniques the counselor uses must correspond to reality,*) is observed in that each of the actions mentioned in this passage are associated with a problem that occurs in real life. At times we can all be unreasonable and be in need of instruction. At times we can all face intense hardship and suffering and need to be comforted. At times we may experience sickness and other disabilities and be in need of help. All of these issues underscore the reality of living in a broken world. Each of the actions Paul prescribes helps us to deal with this reality. A counselor working from a Biblical worldview ought to use techniques that correspond to what is observed in creation.

The seventh characteristic (*counseling techniques given to the counselee ought to be measurable*) is seen in how Paul counseled with the goal of achieving outcomes that were consistent with the grace of God, and one's identity in Christ. For the one who was unruly, instruction was to be given so that they would cease being disorderly. For the person who was fainthearted, encouragement was given to provide them strength and comfort during a time of difficulty. For the individual who was disabled or sick, help was given to them. These are actions that deal directly with the problem at hand. When a counselor operating from a Biblical view uses counseling techniques, these techniques ought to address the problem directly and effectively, as Paul modeled.

The eighth quality (*the counseling techniques ought to be grounded in a proper philosophy and worldview*) is seen in how Paul's philosophy was informed by the Old Testament.[24] Paul was convinced that the Old Testament texts were given by God for humanity's instruction.[25] The prescriptions that Paul wrote were not given to the people of Thessalonica simply because they were convenient, or because they were pragmatic. These instructions were given because they were guided by the reality that God exists, that He is the true God, and that He has given humanity the wisdom to lead intentional lives. For the person counseling from a Biblical worldview these techniques work because they are grounded in truth. They reflect a God who by His very nature is truth.[26]

In the Old Testament account Jethro counseled Moses, demonstrating eight particular qualities of counseling technique. In the same way the New Testament record shows, in Paul's instruction of the

---

[24] c.f., Philippians 4:5-6.
[25] 2 Timothy 3:16.
[26] Psalm 31:5, Isaiah 65:16.

Thessalonians, the value of those same eight qualities. Because of the wisdom presented in these Scriptures, counselors neglecting these eight qualities in their own counseling techniques are less equipped to discern whether or not their techniques are worthwhile for counseling.

PROBLEMATIC USE OF COUNSELING TECHNIQUES BASED ON WORLDVIEW: A CASE STUDY

The counseling model known as *Rebirthing-Breathwork* provides an example of how counseling techniques can be negatively influenced by worldview. The model was created by Lenard Orr, who describes breathwork in this way,

> Rebirthing-Breathwork, aka Intuitive Energy Breathing or Conscious Energy Breathing, is the ability to breathe Energy as well as air. It is the art of learning to breathe from the Breath Itself. Rebirthing is perhaps the most valuable self-healing ability that humans can learn. We can not have disease and relaxation in the same space at the same time. Relaxation is the ultimate healer. Every breath induces relaxation. Therefore, breathing is the basic healer. Conscious Energy Breathing is the most natural healing ability of all. This ability involves merging the inhale with the exhale in a gentle relaxed rhythm in an intuitive way that floods the body with Divine Energy.[27]

Rebirthing-Breathwork found its origins in what is known as Transpersonal Psychology. Transpersonal Psychology came out of the objection Abraham Maslow and others in the psychological community

---

[27] Grof, Stanislav. "Brief History of Transpersonal Psychology." *International Journal of Transpersonal Studies* 27, no. 1 (2008): 46–54. https://doi.org/10.24972/ijts.2008.27.1.46.

had that the discipline of psychology did not cover areas that were unique to humanity:

> [Behaviorism] thus has no relevance for the understanding of higher, specifically human qualities that are unique to human life, such as love, self-consciousness, self-determination, personal freedom, morality, art, philosophy, religion, and science. It is also largely useless in regard to some specifically human negative characteristics, such as greed, lust for power, cruelty, and tendency to "malignant aggression." He also criticized the behaviorists' disregard for consciousness and introspection and their exclusive focus on the study of behavior.[28]

Abraham Maslow and others concluded that the discipline of psychology lacked the research and study in spiritual matters. To address this problem and to fill the gap within the field of psychology, they turned to Eastern religious practices and concepts.[29] In 1967 Abraham Maslow and a group of other practitioners coined the phrase *Transpersonal Psychology*.[30]

One technique of *Rebirthing-Breathwork* involved a subject sitting in a bathtub and processing intense childhood emotional memories. The process of *Rebirthing-Breathwork* was developed further to include water immersion, which according to Lenard Orr symbolized a baby in the womb. Orr developed his breath work in what he described as Conscious Breathing, outside the environment of water, believing this technique assists in the health and well-being of the individual.

In comparison to the eight qualities modeled in the Scriptures, *Rebirthing-Breathwork* presents some problems. According to Orr, *Rebirthing-Breathwork* addresses personal trauma, which can be a presenting

---

[28] Ibid.
[29] Ibid.
[30] Ibid.

problem for some counselees. Some of the types of counseling Lenard Orr describes in his "eight biggies of human trauma:"

> Rebirthing also means to unravel the birth-death cycle and to incorporate the body and mind into the conscious Life of the Eternal Spirit – to become a conscious expression of the Eternal Spirit. This involves healing the eight biggies of human trauma, which are the birth trauma, the parental disapproval syndrome, specific negatives, the unconscious death urge, karma from past lives, the religion trauma, the school trauma, and senility, etc.[31]

In this statement, the second quality of counseling techniques is acknowledged but applied inconsistently, as Orr in the *objective* problems mentioned (e.g., trauma resulting from religion, school, and being senile). However, Orr claims his technique addresses things that are *subjective* to the individual (e.g., parental disapproval syndrome, karma from a previous life, etc.).

Considering the third quality of counseling technique, it is unclear whether or not *Rebirthing-Breathwork* actually addresses the issues that it claims. The techniques originate from Orr's personal experience, which he recounted when he wrote the following,

> The main part of the discovery of Rebirthing took about 10 to 15 years, starting in 1962. The giant leap occurred in 1974-1975. In 1973 I gave a spiritual psychology seminar. There, I talked about the birth memories that I had been having since 1962 in my bathtub and most of the people attending wanted to have birth memories too.[32]

---

[31] "ABOUT: Rebirthing Breathwork International." Rebirthing-Breathwork. Accessed January 3, 2021. https://www.rebirthingbreathwork.com/about.
[32] Ibid.

Due to the lack of clarity that this technique actually addresses the issues of trauma it claims to address, *Rebirthing-Breathwork* fails to demonstrate the third quality of counseling techniques.

Orr's model is instructive to the counselee, however it addresses the issues from a more *personal* and *subjective* nature. This is because the *Rebirthing-Breathwork* is more *experiential* than instructive:

> In 1975, after giving hundreds of hot tub Rebirths, I noticed people having a "healing of the breath" experience. I realized their breathing mechanism was totally transformed and their mind-body-spirit relationship was forever transformed. This healing took place after several sessions — when they felt safe enough to relive the moment of their first breath. Most people feel fear during this moment, so they have to feel safe to reach it.[33]

Because this technique is more experiential than it is informative it fails to show the fourth quality of counseling technique.

Considering the fifth quality, *Rebirthing-Breathwork* does offer a form of practicality: "I found that most people can learn the connected breathing rhythm and how to breathe Energy as well as air in ten two-hour sessions with a good Rebirther."[34] The model does use breathing techniques to assist people in processing traumatic experiences.[35] And research shows the practice of breathing techniques do have a positive effect on the physical body.[36] However when the breathing technique is

---

[33] "ABOUT: Rebirthing Breathwork International." Rebirthing-Breathwork. Accessed January 3,
    2021. https://www.rebirthingbreathwork.com/about.
[34] Ibid.
[35] Ibid.
[36] Decker, James T., Jodi L. Constantine Brown, Wendy Ashley, and Allen E. Lipscom

associated with a philosophy that is *speculative* it is indeterminable whether or not the practice of breathing addresses spiritual problems.

Rebirthing-Breathwork and its philosophy cannot be shown to correspond to reality (the sixth quality). The model is established from the perspective of Transpersonal Psychology, which attempts to address spirituality. The problem is that in this context spirituality is defined and observed by those who are limited in their attributes as human beings, and who can claim no qualification or authority to speak on the spirit. The explanations are limited and insufficient, and the techniques of breathing prescribed in this model are consequently insufficient for addressing spirituality.

Rebirthing-Breathwork, when scrutinized in light of the seventh quality of counseling technique, also falls short. How does one observe or measure if they have been healed or restored from "trauma from past lives?" or even "specific negatives?" Both of these problems Orr describes are vague and subjective in how a counselor would observe and measure the counselee's progress.

Lastly, *Rebirthing-Breathwork,* when observed in light of the eighth quality of counseling technique, betrays several limitations. The model is speculative in how it analyzes the problems it addresses, in the perspective the model has on spirituality, in the foundation of the psychological discipline that undergirds this model, in the promotion of subjective experiences rather than practical information to equip the counselee, in the foundation of the techniques in this model it uses to address these

"Mindfulness, Meditation, and Breathing Exercises: Reduced Anxiety for Clients and Self-Care for
    Social Work Interns." *Social Work with Groups* 42, no. 4 (Oct, 2019): 308-322. doi:http://dx.doi.org.ezproxy.sdcc.edu:2048/10.1080/01609513.2019.1571763. http://ezproxy.sdcc.edu:2048/login?url=https://www-proquest-com.ezproxy.sdcc.edu:2443/scholarly-journals/mindfulness-meditation-breathing-exercises/docview/2287042591/se-2?accountid=25339.

objective and subjective problems, and in the uncertainty of the efficacy of the model to address the problems it claims. In short, *Rebirthing-Breathwork* falls short of corresponding with reality.

OTHER CONSIDERATIONS FOR COUNSELING TECHNIQUE

When it comes to good counseling techniques there are several things worth consideration. First, techniques in counseling may only address physical ailments and relational interaction a person may be experiencing. A person counseling from a Biblical worldview recognizes two things: (1) The curse of the Fall has affected not only the spiritual aspect of humanity, but also the physical aspect of humanity; also, (2) these techniques serve humanity by addressing the physical frailties found in the human body, which underscores creation, and the effect the curse of the Fall has had on the creation itself.

A second consideration is that the *philosophy* that undergirds the technique takes priority over the practice of the technique itself. Paul instructs the saints of Colossae that they were to be cautious of the philosophy that was contrary to the philosophy of Christ.[37] If a counselor who adheres to the Biblical worldview uses bodily awareness and breathing techniques to make a person aware of their own physiological responses, then those can be beneficial, as they can reinforce natural realities, they can underscore the wisdom of God in how humanity is to conduct themselves, and they can meet the qualities for counseling technique. However, if a counselor is convinced that breathing techniques and bodily awareness achieves some higher state of consciousness, or that a counselee may become one with the universe, this is *speculative* worldview thinking and is not consistent with an objective view of reality. This kind of technique application does not meet the qualities of counseling

---

[37] 1 Corinthians 2:14-15.

technique we have been emphasizing (because they are modeled in Scripture).

Third, there are no counseling techniques that are in Scripture that address problems concerning spirituality by personal conduct. Paul explains to the Corinthians that the natural man (*psychikos anthrōpos*) does not receive the words of God that were presented by Paul and the other apostles. In contrast, the one *who is* spiritual (*pneumatikos*) examines all things as it relates to doctrine and yet is examined by no one because this person is convinced of the truth of God.[38] According to the Biblical worldview, spirituality is not determined by how one conducts themselves or their behavior, but by *who they are in Christ*, and their position in the sight of God. When a person believes in Christ, as revealed in Scripture, that person is recognized by God as spiritual. By contrast the one who does not believe in Him is unspiritual (or natural).

CONCLUSION

Counseling is the practice of guiding and instructing counselees. In order to recognize the value of counseling techniques we recognize (at least) eight particular qualities evident in the Old and New Testament. The techniques that are employed in counseling ought to:

1. Investigate to discover the presenting problem
2. Observe the behavior that is counterproductive to the counselee's life
3. Give instruction or information that addresses the counselee's problem specifically
4. Be instructive to the person receiving the counseling
5. Be practical for the counselee

---

[38] 1 Corinthians 2:11-16.

6. Correspond to reality
7. Be measurable
8. Be established within a proper philosophy and worldview

Any technique that fails to model *all* of these qualities fails to meet (at least these) Biblical foundations of psychology and counseling. On the other hand, counselors who are consistently working from these Biblical foundational concepts can be confident that they have something of the greatest value to offer their counselees.

Soli Deo Gloria!

www.ingramcontent.com/pod-product-compliance
Lightning Source LLC
Chambersburg PA
CBHW052129270326
41930CB00012B/2817